Monomotapa
Zulu
Basuto

To Joan, Elena, Tonin, Bev, Jenny, Avril,
Gareth, Giovanna, and many other
friends for their support

FRONT COVER: This rare Zulu doll is covered with intricate beadwork and can be classified as a work of art rather than just a toy.

African Kingdoms of the Past

Monomotapa
Zulu
Basuto
•
Southern Africa

Kenny Mann

Dillon Press • Parsippany, New Jersey

ACKNOWLEDGMENTS

The author wishes to acknowledge the interest, patience, and expertise of the following consultants: Clarence G. Seckel, Jr., Curriculum Coordinator of Social Studies, School District 189. East Saint Louis, IL; Edna J. Whitfield, Social Studies Supervisor (retired), Saint Louis Public Schools, St. Louis, MO.

CREDITS

Design and Illustration: Maryann Zanconato
Picture Research: Kenny Mann and Valerie Vogel

PHOTO CREDITS

All photos by Silver Burdett Ginn unless otherwise noted.
The Bridgeman Art Library: 7. The British Museum/Heini Schneebeli: 61. Bruce Coleman Incorporated/Joan Iaconetti: 29; J. Messerschmidt: 58. Kevin and Anna Conru/Heini Schneebeli: 60. © Hughes Dubois Photographie: Cover, 28. The Hutchison Library: 62–63, 94; Adrian Clark: 80, 85; T.E. Clark: 57; R. Ian Lloyd: 66–67. The Mansell Collection Limited: 39, 90. Museum Africa: 92. National Archives of Zimbabwe: 17, 26, 32, 95. Natural History Photographic Agency/Nigel J. Dennis: 49–49. Peter Newark's Historical Pictures: 45. Photo Researchers, Inc./Clem Haagner: title page; Porterfield/Chickering: 49; H. Von Meiss-Teuffen: 30–31. SBG/Courtesy, The Smithsonian Catalogue: 34. South African Museum/H. Mair: 79. Tony Stone Images/Brian Seed: 9, 98. Maps, Ortelius Design: 6, 25, 36–37, 77.

Library of Congress Cataloging-in-Publication Data
Mann, Kenny.
    Monomotapa, Zulu, Basuto: Southern Africa/ by Kenny Mann.
    p. cm. — (African kingdoms of the past)
    Includes bibliographical references and index.
    ISBN 0-87518-659-9 (LSB). — ISBN 0-382-39300-7 (pbk.)
    1. Africa, Southern—History—To 1899—Juvenile literature. [1. Africa, Southern—History.] I. Title. II. Series.
DT1107.M36   1996   95-45536
968—dc20

Summary: Tracing the history of the African kingdoms of Monomotapa, Zulu, and Basuto, which once occupied the region south of the Zambezi River, this study offers insights into the distinctive cultures of the indigenous peoples of southern Africa and examines how the European powers changed life in the area forever through colonization and conflict.

Published by Dillon Press,
A Division of Simon & Schuster,
299 Jefferson Road, Parsippany, New Jersey 07054

First edition
Printed in the United States of America
10 9 8 7 6 5 4 3 2 1

Table of Contents

African Kingdoms

Note: Dates marked with an * are approximate.

| 30,000 | B.C. | A.D. | 1400 | 1500 | 1600 |

*30,000 B.C.	Stone Age hunter-gatherers occupy Zimbabwe Plateau and veld areas
350 B.C.	Rise of city of Meroe as center of Kushite kingdom in Nile Valley
A.D. 622	Prophet Mohammed founds Islamic faith
*700–1000	Early Iron Age Bantu arrive on Zimbabwe Plateau
*900–1100	Late Iron Age Bantu (Shona) arrive on Zimbabwe Plateau
*1000–1600	Late Iron Age societies (Sotho, Tswana, Nguni, Shona) develop in southern Africa
1003	Vikings reach Vinland (Newfoundland)
*1100	Building of Great Zimbabwe begins
*1420	Nyatsimbe Mutota founds Mutapa kingdom
*1450	Great Zimbabwe abandoned

1480	King Matope of Mutapa dies
1482	Portuguese establish trading fort of El Mina on Guinea coast
1492	Christopher Columbus arrives in the Americas
1493	Songhay kingdom expands in western Sudan
1498	Vasco da Gama rounds the Cape of Good Hope and reaches India
1503	First shipment of African slaves across the Atlantic
1505	Portuguese arrive at Sofala
1511	Antonio Fernandes reaches Chitaka in Mutapa state
1537	Portuguese capture Sena and Tete
1541	First Portuguese settlements in Mutapa state

1629	Portuguese overthrow reigning king and install puppet king; the state becomes a vassal state of Portugal
1652	Dutch arrive at Table Bay and build a fort and a hospital
1693	Changamire raids Mutapa state and drives out Portuguese traders
1760–1770	Boer expansion
1779	First Boer (Xhosa) War
1786	Moshueshue born
1788	Africa Association formed for exploration of continent
1806	British take over Dutch East India Company
1816	Shaka becomes king of the Zulu
1822	Mzilikazi deserts Shaka with 300 followers
1822–1823	The *mfecane*
1823	Moshueshue becomes leader of the Basuto

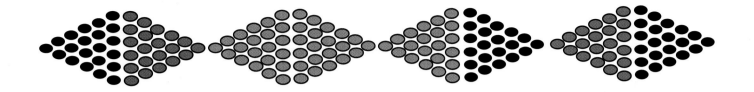

1700	1800	1900	2000

1824–1825	Francis Fynn, Frances Farewell, and Nathaniel Isaacs arrive in Zululand
1828	Shaka assassinated
1830s–1840s	The Great Trek of the Boers
1833	Eugene Casalis meets Moshueshue
1835	British annex, then release, Xhosa territory
1837–1838	Ndebele defeated by Boers; Boers settle in Matabeleland
*1840	Last traces of Mutapa state vanish
1849	David Livingstone crosses Kalahari Desert to Lake Ngami
1850s	Boers claim Orange Free State and Transvaal as Boer republics
1858 and 1865	Boers declare war on the Basuto

1866	Basutoland becomes a British protectorate
1867	American hunter finds ruins of Great Zimbabwe
1869	Borders of modern Lesotho defined; diamonds found at Kimberley
1870	Moshueshue dies; Lobengula becomes king of Ndebele
1872	Cetswayo becomes king of the Zulus
1876	Boers almost bankrupted in Pedi wars
1879–1881	Anglo-Zulu War
1884	European powers divide up Africa at Berlin Congress
1886	Gold found in Transvaal
1887	British annex Zululand to Natal
1890	Pioneer Column reaches Matabeleland
1893–1894	British defeat Ndebele; Lobengula dies
1895	Self-governing colony of Rhodesia founded, administered by British South Africa Company (BSAC)

1896–1897	Ndebele and Shona rebellions in Rhodesia
1899–1902	Anglo-Boer War
1910	Union of South Africa formed
1923	BSAC rule ends in Rhodesia, which becomes a British crown colony
1947	India wins independence from Great Britain
1966	Basutoland becomes independent Kingdom of Lesotho
1980	Rhodesia becomes independent nation of Zimbabwe
1994	Nelson Mandela inaugurated as President of South Africa

Introduction

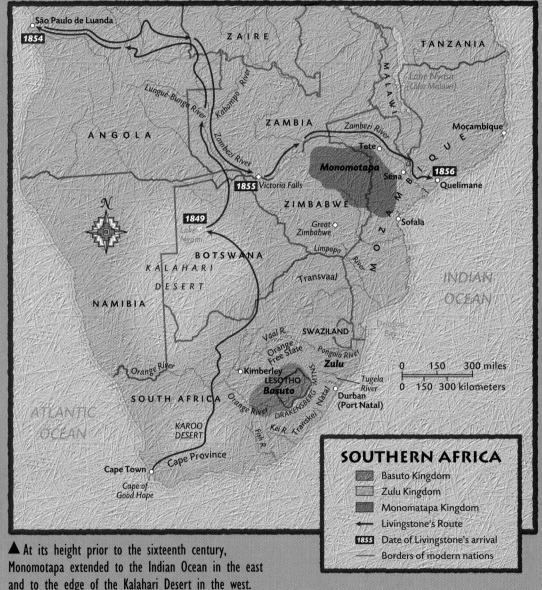

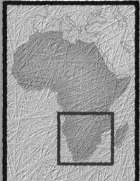

SOUTHERN AFRICA

- Basuto Kingdom
- Zulu Kingdom
- Monomatapa Kingdom
- → Livingstone's Route
- **1855** Date of Livingstone's arrival
- — Borders of modern nations

▲ At its height prior to the sixteenth century, Monomotapa extended to the Indian Ocean in the east and to the edge of the Kalahari Desert in the west.

On Africa's eastern coast, the Zambezi (zam-BEE zee)* River, some 2,700 km (1,700 mi) long, spills into the Indian Ocean between the present-day ports of Beira (BAY rah) and Quelimane (kel ih MAH ne).

The Zambezi River was made famous in the 1850s by the Scottish explorer David Livingstone. Livingstone navigated the river's length and became the first European to cross the African continent from east to west and back again from west to east. Livingstone, a fervent missionary, also hoped to open up the southern continent for European trade, using the great rivers as "pathways" into the interior.

This anonymous portrait of the explorer David Livingstone was painted in 1840, when he was 27 and had just arrived at the Cape.

Livingstone also explored regions south of the Zambezi. In 1849, he traveled north from Cape Town across the Kalahari Desert to Lake Ngami (n GAH mee), now in Botswana. Livingstone recorded his observations and the events along his way in minute detail, leaving us an accurate picture of the regions he saw in the mid-nineteenth century.

The picture that Livingstone offers is very different from the picture an explorer a few hundred years earlier might have provided for his readers. For the indigenous peoples of southern Africa—that is, the part of the continent south of the Zambezi River—had developed distinct ways of life long before the arrival of Europeans, and their lives had undergone many changes in the centuries before Livingstone's expedition.

Over hundreds of years, people of the Bantu language group from areas farther north migrated to southern Africa. Some remained in the arid western

European explorers followed well-established trade routes into the interior. To do so, however, they relied on African guides and servants, and on the hospitality of Africans they met along the way. If some of the Africans who accompanied the great explorers had been able to write their own stories, they might have been as famous as the explorers themselves.

*Words that may be difficult to pronounce have been spelled phonetically in parentheses. A pronunciation key appears on page 99.

Summer south of the equator is from November to March, which is the rainy season in Zimbabwe. A cold, dry winter, which can bring frost and even snow, follows from April to October. The southern and western areas of the plateau are slightly drier than the northern and eastern parts.

Over 450 languages spoken in central and southern Africa have a similar structure and some common words, such as *bantu*—"people," *mvuwa* (m VOO wah)—"rain," and *ndugu* (n DOO goo)—"brother." All these languages probably arose from an ancient language called Bantu by historians today.

regions that make up Namibia today. Others moved farther east, skirting the northern rim of the Kalahari Desert to settle in the region through which Livingstone traveled. Some settled on the coastal plains of the east and southeast, and others on the high plateau of present-day Zimbabwe (zihm BAH bway).

From about A.D. 1000 to 1600, southern Africa experienced a period of profound change. Historians call this period the Late Iron Age. During this time, agricultural and mining practices improved, and tools, utensils, and weapons became more sophisticated. The social structure of the Bantu groups also changed. These changes did not occur at exactly the same time all over the region. In some areas the Late Iron Age began somewhat earlier; in others, somewhat later. Some already existing societies seem to have moved into the new era on their own, while others were clearly influenced by the arrival of newcomers from the north who brought new ideas and techniques with them.

The Bantu developed regional specializations, depending on where they lived. Some were experts in mining, hunting, or metal production. Others were skilled farmers or cattle herders. While these differences encouraged trade between the regions, each group kept its distinctive culture.

Wherever the Bantu moved in southern Africa, they encountered Stone Age hunter-gatherers, known today as the Khoisan (KOI sahn). The Bantu occupied the regions of fairly regular rainfall and either absorbed the Khoisan into their groups or drove them into the arid regions of the southwest, where a few still live today.

With the growth of farming and fishing in the well-watered regions between rivers, the Bantu population grew. People organized themselves into larger groups. These early political units, or clans, needed strong leaders. The early clan heads were almost certainly religious leaders, who had close

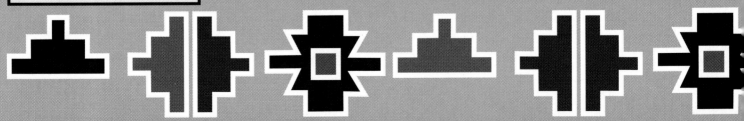

Khoisan: Stone Age hunter-gatherers of the Khoi (sometimes called Khoi-Khoi) and San groups who occupied the southwestern regions of Africa. European colonials in southern Africa rudely referred to the Khoisan as Kaffirs, Bushmen, or Hottentots.

ties to the spiritual world. They may also have controlled trade or had special skills, in metalworking, for instance. Often the early leaders were the "rainmakers" of the clan. They ensured the harvest and were responsible for distributing food in times of drought. They also maintained

A few Khoisan still live in the Kalahari and the arid southwestern regions in small nomadic groups. The men hunt wildebeest and other animals with bows and arrows, and the women collect edible roots, nuts, and berries. ▼

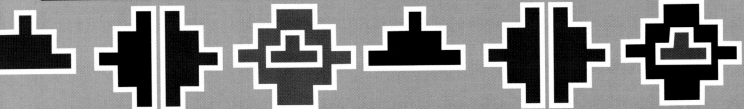

the safety of trade routes, protected people from attack, and organized the move to better grazing or hunting grounds when necessary.

As the Bantu became skilled at using the drier grasslands, cattle became more important. Cattle were a source of milk and, on special occasions only, of meat. They were also traded for iron and other goods, and their leather was used for sandals and shields. But, above all, cattle were, and remain to this day, a source of wealth and power.

When a man wished to marry, he had to pay a dowry of cattle to his bride's father. Those with large herds could afford many wives. All of a man's wives came to live with him. They worked the soil and produced the food. The more wives a man had, the more surplus food he could produce for trade, increasing his wealth even further.

Cattle were cared for exclusively by young boys and men. Although women did not take care of cattle, they produced many sons who did and who added to their father's herds by raiding neighbor-ing groups. Poorer men could borrow cattle from rich neighbors. In this way, wealthy men came to dominate women and poorer men, and large areas of land. These men were the most likely to be selected as leaders or chiefs. Thus, cattle were a prime factor in the development of early chiefdoms in southern Africa. Later, powerful leaders sought to conquer neighboring clans, amass huge herds of cattle, and build their chiefdoms into small states. If these leaders conquered several states, they eventually formed a kingdom.

Not all chiefdoms developed into kingdoms, however, and the factors affecting those that did varied from region to region. Almost always, leaders collected taxes and other payment, or tribute, from their vassal, or subject, states. In some cases a clan's control of trade routes brought it enough wealth to conquer its neighbors and expand its territory. In others, a strong central government was the key to expansion. Sometimes an individual seized power and led a military state. Some strong leaders attracted many followers and founded kingdoms during times of warfare or famine. Other kingdoms arose as protection against European settlement.

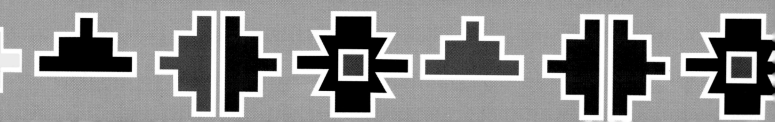

The history of southern Africa's kingdoms was first recorded not by Africans, but by Europeans: Portuguese, Dutch, British, and French traders, soldiers, farmers, and missionaries. Whoever records a people's history has the power to shape their identity. The peoples of southern Africa have struggled to resist the imposition of a foreign identity by outsiders.

In Zimbabwe, Natal, and Lesotho, people today still recall the stories of the old kingdoms of Monomotapa (mohn oh moh TAH pah), Zulu, and Basuto. But these stories were first written down by Europeans. They are descriptions of southern Africa through European eyes. Would the stories have been different if they had first been recorded by Africans? We will never know.

Kupara, seen here in 1956, was a great oral historian of the Monomotapa dynasty and a major source of information for European historians. ▶

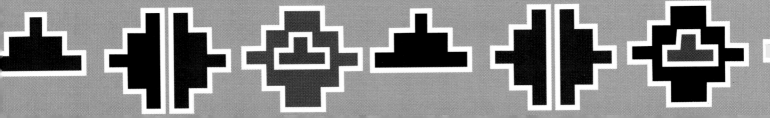

1

MONOMOTAPA

Monomotapa—
The Zambezi Kingdom

Gatsi Rusere: The Collaborator

The great empire of Monomotapa is crossed by an important and large river which the natives call the Zambezi. The kingdoms and lands of the great king of Monomotapa have a circumference of more than 300 leagues. The government of the kingdom is divided among petty chiefs and other lords with fewer vassals, and all are vassals of Gatsi Rusere (GHAT see roo SE re), the king. Besides all these there is also a large main state, called Mokaranga (moh kah RAHN gah), where Gatsi Rusere resides with his court.

The greater part of this empire abounds with gold. It is worthy of note that from a quarry in the mountain of Fura more than 400,000 *cruzados* were extracted in a short time. Some of our Portuguese men saw a vein of gold growing in the pith of a tree trunk, and, digging where the tree stood, they extracted 10,000 or 12,000 *cruzados* in a short time. In some parts, nuggets of natural gold have been found on the surface of the earth, and countless gold fragments, large and small.

In the vast region north of the Zambezi lived a Kaffir (KAF ur) named Chunzo, a powerful king with many subjects. Chunzo envied the great power and authority of Gatsi Rusere. He resolved to make war upon

League: a measure of distance equal to about three miles or almost five kilometers.

Cruzado: a sixteenth-century Portuguese coin bearing an image of the cross.

Kaffir: a Muslim word for "infidels," people who do not believe in Islam. The term was often applied to non-Muslim Africans. The Portuguese adopted the term for all Africans, and it was later used by European settlers in an insulting way.

the king and to win from him the neighboring kingdoms. Therefore, Chunzo chose two of his captains who were very valiant, and sent them in different directions with forces to enter these lands and conquer them. This was in the year of our Lord 1597.

The principal captain, called Capampo, entered lands that are situated along the Zambezi River. He made himself master of them and then attacked other lands, very rich in gold, where the Portuguese merchants go and trade. Gatsi Rusere, knowing the great damage that Capampo was doing in his territories, promptly ordered a large army to be assembled. He made Ningomoxa (nihn goh MOHK suh), his governor and the second in command in his kingdom, the chief captain of this army.

At the same time, the king sent his ambassadors to the Portuguese, who were in Mokaranga, to ask them if they would help to drive Capampo out of Monomotapa. The Portuguese, who wished to trade freely, willingly agreed. They saw the advantages of a land free of robbers, and immediately set out to accompany the king's army, under the leadership of Ningomoxa. Capampo heard of the preparations being made against him and that the Portuguese were armed with guns. He quickly retreated from the region and on the way he burned all the provisions he could find. Our people, the Portugese, who were following him, therefore had

Early European witnesses and historians usually considered themselves and their culture superior to all others. Thus they referred to indigenous peoples as "natives" rather than "inhabitants," "warriors" and "braves" rather than "soldiers," or simply lumped them all under one name, such as "Kaffir." More recent historians try to avoid such value judgments about other peoples, regions, and periods of history.

The founder of the kingdom called himself *Mwene* (m WE ne), the Bantu word for "king." He added the title *Mutapa,* meaning "conqueror." Over time, the king's titles merged to become the name of the kingdom itself—Monomotapa. Modern historians sometimes refer to the kingdom as the Mutapa state.

nothing to eat. Forced by hunger, Ningomoxa ordered them to turn back and abandon their pursuit of the enemy. Gatsi Rusere was so enraged at this that he ordered Ningomoxa to be put to death, although he was his uncle and the second in command in his kingdom; and from Ningomoxa's death arose all the evils that afterwards fell on the king.

The second of Chunzo's captains was called Chicanda. He penetrated a different part of the country where many slaves of the Portuguese acted as traders. Defeating and robbing them of everything, he passed on and took up a position along the Motambo River, which is near the king's court, in the heart of Monomotapa. Fearing that Gatsi Rusere might attack and destroy him, Chicanda sent ambassadors to the king with a rich present. They told Gatsi Rusere that Chicanda had entered the kingdom of Monomotapta without the king's leave, for which Chicanda asked pardon. But his intention in doing so, the ambassadors said, was to serve Gatsi Rusere and to be his vassal rather than that of Chunzo. And Chicanda begged the king to accept him as such and grant him leave to settle in these lands.

Gatsi Rusere allowed Chicanda to settle according to his desire. Here Chicanda remained quietly for two years. But at the end of this period he rebelled against Monomotapa and began to attack some of the lands belonging to the king's wives, which were close by. Chicanda caused such destruction in the area that Gatsi Rusere was obliged to ask again for help from the Portuguese.

The inhabitants of Sena (SE nah) and Tete (te te), our Portugese settlements along the Zambezi River, arranged to assist the king, both to please him and to avenge the thefts and losses they had suffered through the rebel Chicanda. Seventy-five Portuguese and 2,000 Kaffirs assembled at Tete and set out toward Chicanda's fort.

They found it surrounded by 30,000 of the king's fighting men. But Chicanda, who had only 600 men, attacked the Monomotapa forces by day and by night, killing and wounding them.

Our Portuguese and the Kaffir's men encamped near the fort. It was very high—built of thick, strong wood surrounded by a trench. A wall of earth taken from the trench was banked very high against the walls, which had holes for arrows. Our people made large wickerwork screens, open at the back and covered at the top, which could shield 50 Kaffirs. The Kaffirs carried the screens before them like a wall until they reached Chicanda's fort, remaining unharmed by the enemy's arrows. There were holes in these screens, through which our Kaffirs discharged their arrows and the Portuguese their guns, and in this manner they reached and attacked the fort and then filled up the trench.

The battle lasted from morning until night. Chicanda, seeing that he was almost defeated, asked the Portuguese to promise him and his men their lives and then they would surrender. Their offer, however, was not accepted because Gatsi Rusere wished to rid his land of Chicanda and his mob. An answer was returned that the next day the punishment they deserved would be completed.

On hearing this reply Chicanda and his men did not wait for the morrow but sallied out of the fort at dead of night and fled. Many were killed in the attempt. Our people sent word to Gatsi Rusere of what they had done. He sent them his thanks for the service they had rendered him and said they might return to their homes. Upon this answer, the Portuguese took leave of the Monomotapa soldiers— their brothers in arms—and set out for Tete. And from that time forth, Gatsi Rusere allowed the Portuguese to enter his country with guns, which had been strictly forbidden by him before.

The Portuguese called Monomotapa an empire, but it was really one large state ruled by the members of one dynasty. At times, outlying states were vassals of the central state, paying tribute and acknowledging the king's authority. But such arrangements changed when states rebelled and became independent or as new states were added. The location of the capital city often shifted, depending on rainfall, the availability of food for the large population, and relations with neighboring states.

The Lure Of Gold

This description of Monomotapa—the kingdom located in what is today Zimbabwe (formerly Southern Rhodesia)—is adapted from accounts written by Antonio Bocarro, who was Keeper of the Archives for King Philip III of Portugal from 1631 until his death around 1649. Bocarro was one of the many chroniclers who were employed by the Portuguese kings to record events wherever the Portuguese had holdings.

The Portuguese had long heard from Muslim traders about the rich goldfields of southeast Africa's interior. In the tenth century an Arab historian named al Masudi had written of a certain gold-producing kingdom west of the port of Sofala (soh FAH-lah). And in 1498, on his journey of exploration around the Cape of Good Hope to India, Vasco da Gama had also received news of Monomotapa.

By the fifteenth century, Swahili (swah HEE lee) traders from the East African coast had established trading relationships with people living far inland along the Zambezi. These people were skilled at cotton weaving, ivory carving, and metalwork in copper, gold, and iron, and traded the goods they made for beads and cloth. In 1505 the Portuguese landed at Sofala. Determined to seize control of the Swahili trade, they built a fort there (and later one at Mozambique) that was to be the "gateway to the land of gold." Soon, African traders arrived, claiming that the great king of Monomotapa "owned" all the gold of the region. They had come to establish peaceful relations with the foreigners and probably to impress them with their king's power.

> **Muslim:**
> a follower of Islam, the religious faith founded by the prophet Mohammed in A.D. 622

By 1511 a traveler named Antonio Fernandes had followed the well-worn trade route from Sofala to the king's court at Chitaka (chih TAH kah), located on a tributary of the Zambezi. He was the first European ever to set foot in the area, which is now part of Zimbabwe.

The king gave Fernandes permission to travel throughout the kingdom, and

Fernandes found that the stories of gold were indeed true. "One man," he wrote, "says he can see where the gold lies because an herb like clover grows over it." Fernandes reported that he saw mined in one day "a large basket full of [gold] bars the size of a finger and large nuggets." This was all the encouragement the Portuguese needed. With their arrival in the interior, the kingdom of Monomotapa was to embark on a 300-year-long battle for survival.

The Founding of Monomotapa

Bocarro reported that within the kingdom of Monomotapa was a "principal state" called Mokaranga where the king lived. The people of this area were known as the Karanga and belonged to a large Bantu language group called the Shona (SHOH nuh).

◀ Through the Portuguese, Monomotapa became well known in sixteenth-century Europe and was included on maps made by Europeans. Dutch and French artists who had never visited Africa drew their impressions of the Monomotapa kings. In this portrait the king has been given a crown and a scepter, the symbols of power of European kings. Historians still debate whether this was out of respect or ignorance.

The Portuguese reported that the king was always concealed behind a curtain where he could be heard but not seen. Visitors had to crawl toward the king on their bellies. If he coughed, everyone coughed. If he sprained his ankle, everyone limped. Were these reports exaggerated? No one knows.

According to Karanga oral tradition, the kingdom of Monomotapa was founded in about 1420 by Mutota (moo TOH tah), a strong leader from an area farther south. Apparently, supplies of salt in that region had been used up, and Mutota and his people were forced to move north to find new sources of salt. Mutota and his followers settled in the gold-rich Dande (DAHN de) region, near the head of the Mazoe (mah ZOH ee) River. The area was fertile and offered plenty of wood for building. There was also easy access to the Zambezi River and the trading centers of Sena and Tete. On the coast itself, the town of Sofala had long been established as a trading center where Arabs, Africans, and possibly even Indians and Chinese came to exchange their wares for gold and ivory.

Mutota's son and successor, Matope (mah TOH pe), set about expanding the state. Through a series of brilliant military maneuvers, he conquered the many smaller states lying between the Kalahari and the Indian Ocean. Matope organized an efficient government with different levels of power, which was run by his sons and nephews. He also followed a system that was widespread in the Bantu regions of Africa, in which goods brought from one area to another were taxed. In addition, vassal states had to pay the king tribute of various kinds. The revenues from taxes and tribute supported an army and the king's household, which often numbered in the thousands.

The kingdom that Antonio Fernandes visited in the early sixteenth century occupied a huge area between the Zambezi and Limpopo rivers. Most of the kingdom lay on high land some 914 m (3,000 ft) above sea level that is known today as the Zimbabwe Plateau. The kingdom had no clearly defined borders, but historians estimate that its northern boundary was probably formed by the Zambezi River. The Hunyani (hoon YAH nee) River, a tributary of the Zambezi, probably formed the western boundary.

The blind and maimed in the kingdom were called "the king's poor" and were given food and drink at the public expense wherever they went. They also received land for their families. When traveling, a guide ensured that they arrived safely and were not robbed. Any person failing to fulfill these obligations to the blind was punished by the king.

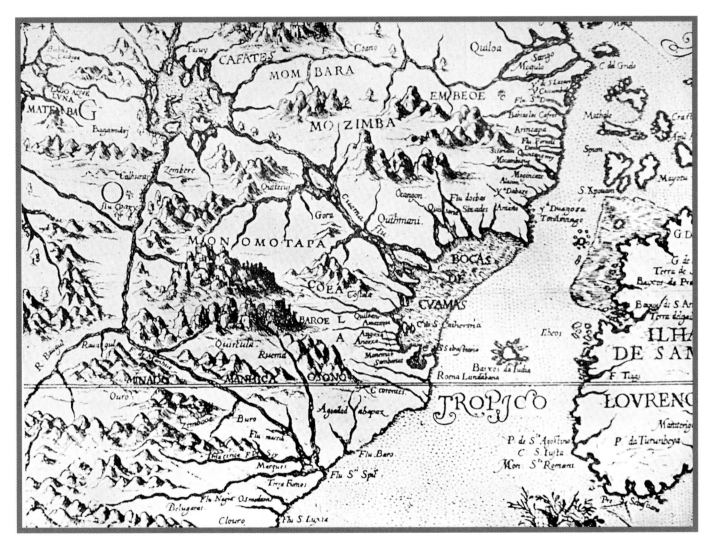

▲ This sixteenthth-century map clearly shows the kingdom of Monomotapa and the sea channel between Madagascar and the coast. The map is taken from the report compiled by Antonio Fernandes, the first European to set foot in the kingdom. At its height, prior to the sixteenth century, Monomotapa extended to the Indian Ocean in the east and to the edge of the Kalahari Desert in the west.

The king was waited on by many officers, who had specific duties. The kingdom had a governor and a chief majordomo, responsible for naming a successor to the king's chief wife when she died and for handling her estate. The chief musician, a "very great lord," directed hundreds of court musicians. Among the many other officers were a captain of the vanguard in time of war; a chief wizard; the king's apothecary, who kept his charms and medicines; and even a chief doorkeeper.

The Hunyani eventually joined the Matzoe (mah ZOH ee), which flowed into the Zambezi.

The Karanga people lived in simple dwellings made of poles and plastered with mud called *dagga* (DAH gah), with thatched roofs. The kings, however, lived on a grander scale. Portuguese records describe very large, beautifully constructed solid *dagga* huts surrounded by elaborate stone walls or high wooden stockades. The Portuguese referred to some of these settlements as cities or large towns with populations of between 1,000 and 2,000 people.

As in many other African kingdoms, the king enjoyed enormous power. He had many wives, who were held in very high esteem. In fact, the word *karanga* means "wife," and even powerful male officials in the kingdom could receive the honorary title of "great wife." The king's wives were powerful individuals who par-

ticipated in politics and played an important role in the struggles for succession when a king died. Each wife had her own estate, lands, and servants, and sometimes even her own army. When a wife died, another wife inherited her estate and duties.

The king and his court lived in relative splendor. Some kings wore the finely worked skins of leopards or wild cats, "trailing along the ground like tails, [the kings] making leaps and gestures to

"Young nobles between the ages of 15 and 20 are employed to lay the food when the king wishes to eat, which they spread upon . . . a carpet or mat, with muslin extended above, and many different kinds of meat are set before him, all roasted or boiled, such as hens, pigeons, partridge, capons, sheep, venison, hares, rabbits, cows, rats, and other game, of which, after the king has eaten, a portion is given to some of his servants who are always provided from his table."
—Antonio Bocarro, 1631–1649

make those tails go from one side to the other," according to a Portuguese trader in 1518. Others dressed in the clothing of wealthy Muslims from the East African coastal cities. They wore a cloth wound around the waist and reaching to their feet, with another cloth thrown over their shoulders as a cape. Some kings wore silks, satins, damask, or embroidered cloth of gold decorated with ribbons. These were imported from India and the Far East. Despite their status, the Monomotapa kings moved freely among their people, hunting or going to war with their soldiers. When he left his palace, the king was preceded by a man beating a special instrument to warn people of his coming.

King Matope died around 1480, leaving a weak successor who struggled to hold the kingdom together. Only a few years later, the Portuguese arrived, adding their own agenda to the already complicated political scene in Monomotapa.

The Portuguese In Monomotapa

By 1528, adventurous Portuguese individuals had begun to trade in the interior of southern Africa. In the 1530s they sent a small army up the Zambezi and captured the Swahili trading posts of Sena and Tete. But no Portuguese settlement is recorded until 1541, when the *mutapa* himself invited official Portuguese representatives to settle within his domain. These officers, known as the Captains of the Gates, were selected by the Portuguese but came under the authority of the *mutapa*.

At first, the Portuguese planned to pay tribute to the king for permission to trade within his territory. But they were legally permitted to buy only very small amounts of gold, and so they became determined to gain control of the kingdom and operate the gold mines themselves. This idea

Traders used very light, long boats called *almadias* (ahl mah DEE-ahs) to carry goods up the Zambezi to Sena, where about 30 Portuguese traders lived with their slaves. From Sena, the merchants transported goods overland to marketplaces or *feiras* (FAY rahs) in the south and in Monomotapa to the west, where they traded them for gold.

was to fuel Portuguese efforts in the area right up to the late nineteenth century.

From the start the Portuguese faced huge difficulties. First, they were very few in number—perhaps only 200 within the entire region at any one time. Along the Zambezi River, they faced hostile rulers. In addition, the Europeans suffered from and often died of tropical diseases like malaria. And the area was prone to long-lasting periods of terrible drought, when many people starved to death. Not only this but the fabled gold mines proved disappointing. African miners had already extracted what they could with their own technology, and European technology was not much more advanced.

The Portuguese trading captains placed expensive bids for their positions and then bought the monopoly of trade along the Zambezi for periods of three years. They also had to pay a high tax to the king. In the sixteenth and seventeenth centuries, this huge initial investment was justified by profits of 100 to 400 percent.

Nevertheless, the Portuguese maintained a strong interest in trading with Monomotapa because they could receive ivory, gold, and cloth, which were extremely valuable on the international market, in exchange for items such as guns, beads, and metal utensils, which were of far less value internationally. Inevitably the Portuguese became deeply involved in African politics, placing their loyalties where it most suited them.

As Antonio Bocarro faithfully reported, the execution of Gatsi Rusere's uncle and commanding officer, Ningomoxa, caused a civil war as rivals battled for the throne. By this time, individual Portuguese traders had penetrated inland, set up their own fortified settlements, and recruited large armies of African troops. In 1629, these troops helped to overthrow the reigning king and place his rival on the throne. In return for their help, the Portuguese demanded huge concessions. The new king had to give them the rights to all the gold, silver, and iron mines of the kingdom. They were no longer accountable to the king's laws for anything they did. And worst of all, the African king was made a vassal of the king of Portugal.

Needless to say, these affairs caused great resentment among the Karanga people and those who laid claim to the throne. As a result, there were several uprisings, which caused the internal struggles between the Portuguese and the Monomotapa kings to continue for another 250 years.

Monomotapa was severely weakened by the Portuguese. In 1693 and 1702, the kingdom was challenged by a serious rival from the south-west. The man who threatened the kingdom was named Changamire (chan gah MEE re). He had built up a formidable army of warriors known as the Rozvi (ROHZ vee), who drove the Portuguese out of their territory in 1690. The Changamire state dominated most of the plateau, including some former territories of the Mutapa, for 100 years. By 1840, however, new world trade routes had opened up, causing a decrease in Indian Ocean trade. Without trade, the Changamire state collapsed.

Some historians claim that the Portuguese "conquered" Monomotapa in the battle of 1629. Others believe that Changamire's raids caused the kingdom's downfall. Still others observe that the central state of the kingdom did in fact survive until about 1840. The African historian S. Mudenge (moo DEN ge) suggests that present-day Zimbabwe represents a direct geographical, cultural, and political link to ancient Monomotapa. If this is so, Zimbabweans today may find a solid foundation for their future in their past.

The Zimbabwe Plateau

Most of Zimbabwe lies on the Zimbabwe Plateau, which stretches from the Zambezi River in the north to the Limpopo River in the south. The hot, low-lying Zambezi Valley extends along the northeastern, northern, and northwestern boundaries of the Plateau. To the east, the Plateau spreads down through woodlands to the Indian Ocean. To the south lies the Limpopo with its dry valley, and to the southwest, the Plateau spreads gradually into the Kalahari. Mountain ranges in the northwest and the east reach altitudes of over 1,500 m (5,000 ft). Many rivers and their tributaries bisect the Plateau, cutting deep swaths through the granite rock. In between, a savannah-woodland covers the plains,

thickening to deep woods on the mountains and thinning to sparse brush in the valleys.

The history of the Shona people has played itself out against this spectacular landscape for almost 2,000 years. The Shona still inhabit large areas of the Plateau, in what is now Zimbabwe. They were not the first people to settle on the Plateau, however. From about 30,000 B.C., Late Stone Age hunter-gatherers lived in this area. They left behind some of their tools and weapons—mainly stone axes and arrowheads. These objects and ancient rock paintings suggest that these early people were like the present-day Khoisan of the

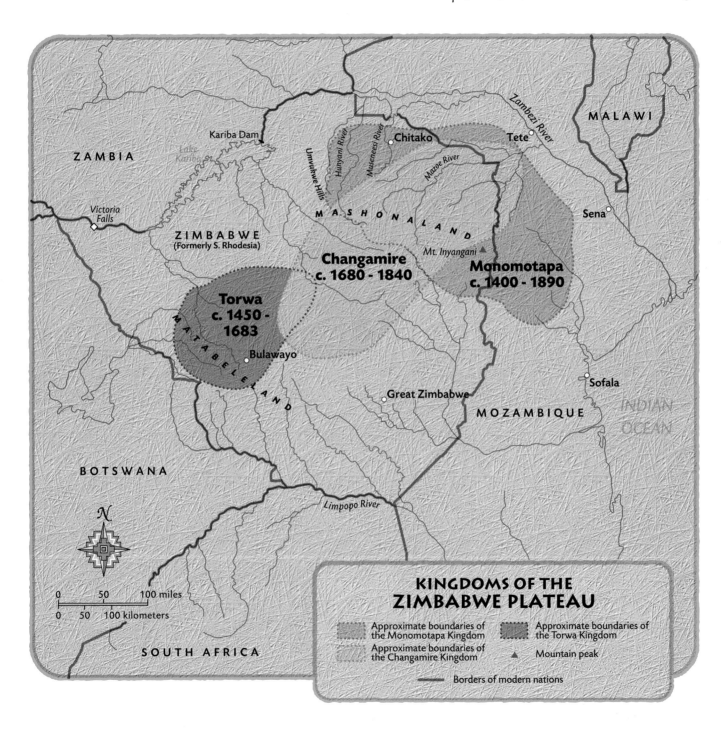

ZAMBIA

Kariba Dam

Lake Kariba

Victoria Falls

ZIMBABWE
(Formerly S. Rhodesia)

Unvukwe Hills

Hunyani River

Museneesi River

Chitako

Mazoe River

Zambezi River

Tete

MALAWI

M A S H O N A L A N D

Sena

Changamire
c. 1680 - 1840

Mt. Inyangani ▲

Monomotapa
c. 1400 - 1890

Torwa
c. 1450 -
1683

M A T A B E L E L A N D

Bulawayo

Great Zimbabwe

Sofala

MOZAMBIQUE

INDIAN OCEAN

BOTSWANA

N

Limpopo River

| 0 | 50 | 100 miles |
| 0 | 50 | 100 kilometers |

SOUTH AFRICA

KINGDOMS OF THE ZIMBABWE PLATEAU

Approximate boundaries of the Monomotapa Kingdom

Approximate boundaries of the Torwa Kingdom

Approximate boundaries of the Changamire Kingdom

▲ Mountain peak

Borders of modern nations

Some time around 350 B.C. small groups of Bantu - speaking people began moving south from the area of present-day Cameroon in search of new lands. They were ironworkers, looking for iron ore and plenty of wood for their smelting fires. With the iron, they made weapons and agricultural tools. They also made clay pots. Different groups developed distinctive styles of pottery. Pottery shards, remains of ancient coal fires and of crop storage systems, and language studies have enabled archaeologists and linguists to trace Bantu movements across the continent. Some Bantu peoples, like these women, still decorate their pots in the styles developed during the Late Iron Age. ▶

southwest. They were short, yellow-skinned rather than black, and moved about the land in small groups, following the grazing patterns of wild animals and the cycle of rainy and dry seasons.

Then, quite suddenly, the archaeological evidence shows the arrival of two new groups of people. Unlike the Khoisan, these people knew how to mine and smelt iron and forge iron tools and weapons. They probably drove the Khoisan out of the area or intermarried with them. With iron axes they were able to clear the ground, and with iron hoes they could prepare fields for crops. They were now less dependent on hunting and the seasons and could remain in one area for longer periods. They could cut trees and use the wood for fires and for building huts, which they covered with *dagga*.

These people also introduced pottery—a major innovation for carrying, storing, and cooking food and water. Each group created its own pottery style of shape and decoration. The shards, or pieces, they left behind offer valuable clues about these groups and their relations with one another.

There is little doubt that the first group, who arrived between A.D. 700 and 1000, were Early Iron Age Bantu, who had been moving south from the forests of central Africa since about A.D. 500. But it is also certain that they were not Shona speakers. People who did speak Shona appear to have arrived in a migratory second wave, indicated by the sudden introduction of a completely new style of pottery. This change occurred around

Archaeological evidence indicates that the early Shona settlers approached the Zimbabwe Plateau from the south. But Shona oral tradition holds that they came from the north. The story goes that Murenga Sororenzou headed the first ancestral family to arrive on the Plateau. One of his children was Nehanda. She died before crossing the Zambezi. Her spirit took possession of a medium who, just like Moses, parted the raging waters of the great river with a wooden staff so that Nehanda's followers could cross. Nehanda is revered to this day as one of the great ancestor spirits of the Shona people.

The Shona month consisted of 30 days, from the first day of the new moon to the last day of that moon, and was divided into 3 weeks of 10 days each. In each week, the fourth and seventh days of the moon were holidays, making 6 in a month.

On the first day of the new moon, the king held a great feast attended by all his nobles and vassals. On the eighth day of the moon in May, the king executed a noble, who was offered as a sacrifice to the ancestors. In this way the king continually reinforced his power and authority.

A.D. 900 in the south, and around A.D. 1100 in the north, and leads to the conclusion that the new group must have moved over the Plateau from south to north.

Bones found at several sites indicate that large numbers of cattle also appeared at this time. Clay figurines of cattle, unlike anything found earlier, also became common. Cattle could thrive on the high plateau because it was free of the tsetse fly, which bred at lower altitudes and carried a deadly disease. The appearance of cattle signifies a major change in the regional economy and in the structure of society. Archaeologists believe that these Late Iron Age people were Shona, who conquered, drove out, or absorbed the earlier inhabitants.

Great Zimbabwe

In 1867 an American hunter named Adam Renders claimed to have found the remains of immense stone fortresses or palaces hidden in the southeastern corner of the Zimbabwe Plateau. Soon after, a German geologist named Frobenius (froh BAY nee us) visited the ruins and came to the extraordinary conclusion that they were the ruins of King Solomon's temple in the fabled land of Ophir (OH fihr)—the source of Solomon's gold!

The very mention of gold was enough to send European fortune hunters scurrying. By 1900, about 114,000 gold claims had been registered in and around the ruins, mostly where ancient mines had already sunk their shafts into the ground. The ruins were damaged and looted of thousands of invaluable artifacts. Two years later the government of what was then Southern Rhodesia put a stop to the vandalism, and in 1905, serious archaeological study of the ruins began.

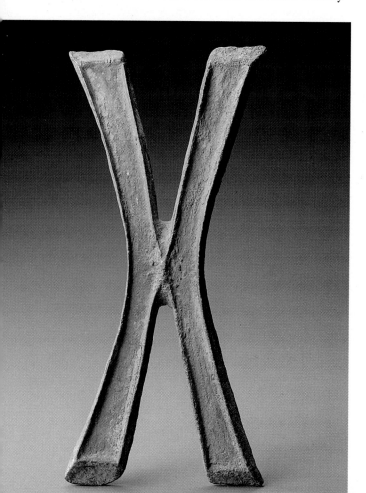

◀ Copper was mined from deposits north and south of the Zambezi River, and was an important source of wealth. This copper ingot was found at a fifteenth-century burial site in the Zambezi Valley. Ingots shaped like this one could be easily carried by bearers using shoulder sticks.

The name *Zimbabwe* comes from the Shona term *dzimba dzamabwe* (DZEEM bah dzah MAH bway), meaning "stone buildings." The ruins that Adam Renders had found were named Great Zimbabwe.

Great Zimbabwe is an extensive complex of stone walls. In a wooded valley stands a single large enclosure that historians call the Elliptical Building, because of its shape. In some places the enclosure's outer wall is 11 m (35 ft) high and 5 m (17 ft) thick. From within this wall rises what is known as the Conical Tower. The tower is huge and similar in shape to Shona grain storehouses. Surrounding the Elliptical Building are several smaller enclosures of similar shape. Across the valley, on top of a granite cliff, stands another high-walled enclosure called the Hill Ruin. And in the valleys and on the plains for miles around can be found the ruins of many smaller *zimbabwe*.

Untold strength and labor must have gone into the construction of these walls. Their stones were perfectly cut from the granite of the surrounding hills and arranged in complex patterns and curves without the use of nails, pegs, or

▲ The great wall of the Eliptical Building, which is more than 250 m (820 ft) long, surrounds the Conical Tower at Great Zimbabwe. Skilled stonemasons built the wall, the tower, and other structures without using mortar or nails.

mortar. Who built Great Zimbabwe? What was it for? Why is it the only complex of its kind in Africa? Over the last century, scholars have pieced together much of the history of the area. But an air of deep mystery still surrounds this extraordinary relic of the past.

Carbon dating has confirmed that Great Zimbabwe was not built all at one time but rather over a period of about 350 years, beginning in about A.D. 1100 and ending around A.D. 1450. Construction became more sophisticated as time went on.

The walls that remain today once surrounded private family compounds containing many dwellings. The Elliptical Building

Shona Manners
To enter someone else's dwelling, a visitor stands outside and shouts "Gogogoyi!", which means "Knock, knock, knock."

To receive a gift, a person first claps their hands together in a gesture of thanks. No matter how small, the gift is taken with both hands to show that it is too large for one hand only.

◀ The Conical Tower is thought to have represented the king's power. Surrounding the king's dwelling were the lesser stone buildings of the members of his court, and spread over about 40 hectares (100 acres) were the pole and *dagga* dwellings of farmers and craftworkers. Their huts left no traces, but their rubbish heaps of ash, bones, and household debris provide clues about their occupations and ways of life.

probably surrounded the dwelling place of a king or powerful leader. It was not intended as a fortress but perhaps simply signified the status and power of the king. Great Zimbabwe does not look like a city. There are no streets or marketplaces, no communal, industrial, or commercial buildings. Yet the evidence shows that at its peak between 5,000 and 11,000 people must have occupied the site and its surrounding lands.

Clearly, Great Zimbabwe arose out of a sophisticated society that had the technology to build its walls. It is located in an area of fairly reliable rainfall, wide rivers, and fertile plains, ideal for hunting, breeding cattle, and growing crops. Very early Shona settlers probably managed to gain command over this territory. They must have had more cattle than other settlers, thus attracting more wives and followers than their rivals. Yet cattle breeding and agriculture alone could not have led them to develop a prosperous state with a capital at Great Zimbabwe. Nor could the nearby gold mines, which gave very poor yields, could have done so.

A thousand years ago, sculptors carved soapstone images of birds on the walls of Great Zimbabwe, perhaps to link the site with the heavens above. The bird, shown with a carved crocodile climbing the pole on which it perches, is now the national emblem of Zimbabwe. ▶

Recent work has shown that Great Zimbabwe probably lay on an important trade route linking settlements farther west—which were extremely rich in gold—to the port of Sofala in the east. The rulers of Great Zimbabwe must have become wealthy and powerful by imposing heavy taxes on the gold from the west and on iron and ivory, the other trading commodities passing from west to east through their domain. They would also have taxed the cloth, beads, and other items that were traded from east to west.

Pottery, iron tools and weapons, soapstone bowls, and gold jewelry found at Great Zimbabwe show that it was a center of crafts and industry. One archaeological site yielded pieces of coral, bronze hawk bells, cowrie shells, shards of Chinese porcelain, Syrian glass, a Persian bowl bearing an Arabic inscription, an iron spoon and lampstand, and copper chains whose origins remain unknown.

From these clues we know that Great Zimbabwe—far from being isolated in the African bush—was well connected to a vast international trade network. It had

In African societies, women generally are responsible for fetching water and firewood and tending to the fields. As Great Zimbabwe grew in size and population, more land was cleared for farming. Women would have had to walk even longer distances to collect wood and reach the fields. Perhaps the Shona abandoned the site because the women simply had to walk too far to work!

bound the Far East, India, the Persian Gulf, and the East African coast to its expanding economy for centuries. Contemporary historian Peter Garlake even suggests that Indian traders, searching the East African coast for new sources of iron and gold, may have brought their mining know-how to the Plateau as early as the fourth century A.D. Indonesians who had settled on the Indian Ocean island of Madagascar very probably also traded with and influenced the people of Zimbabwe. Perhaps, Garlake proposes, the enclosure at Great Zimbabwe was a holding ground for slaves captured in the interior. They would eventually have

The Trade Network

The Shona were mainly agriculturalists. They mined and traded to survive in times of drought or hardship. Gold was their main export, but because the mineral was so hard to obtain, ivory became more important in international trade. Elephants were trapped in pits or hunted with spears. African ivory was popular in India because it was softer than Indian ivory and could be worked into much-prized jewelry and ornaments. High-quality African iron was also used in India to make steel for swords and other weapons. Copper and ostrich feathers were exported to India and the Persian Gulf.

Indian cotton was the major import to the Plateau, along with dyed and embroidered silk, satin, and damask. With these fabrics came the techniques of weaving and spinning. Eventually the quality of Shona cloth surpassed that of the Indian imports. As early as A.D. 700, agate and carnelian beads were also imported from northern India. They were later replaced by glass beads brought by Arab and Portuguese traders. The kingdom of Monomotapa also had trading relationships with areas located today in Mozambique, southeastern Zambia, Malawi, Botswana, northern Transvaal (South Africa), Tanzania, and possibly even Angola.

been transported to the huge date plantations of Mesopotamia in what is today Iraq.

Great Zimbabwe reached its peak of prosperity in the fourteenth century. Yet by 1505, when the Portuguese arrived, it had already been abandoned. Although no one knows what happened to Great Zimbabwe, historians guess that the growth of the state led to its downfall. The land around Great Zimbabwe simply could not support the increasing number of people living there. In addition, the Zimbabwe state was at the mercy of international trade and had used up its own valuable resources—gold, iron, and slaves—exchanging them for almost worthless trinkets and luxury items. And so Great Zimbabwe—considered one of the wonders of the world—sank into ruin, leaving its secrets for historians to ponder for generations to come.

◀When Great Zimbabwe was abandoned, the art of sculpting seems to have vanished. It was revived in the 1960s by Shona sculptors. Their work is now famed throughout the world and has been exhibited in major art museums. This contemporary piece represents the unity of the family.

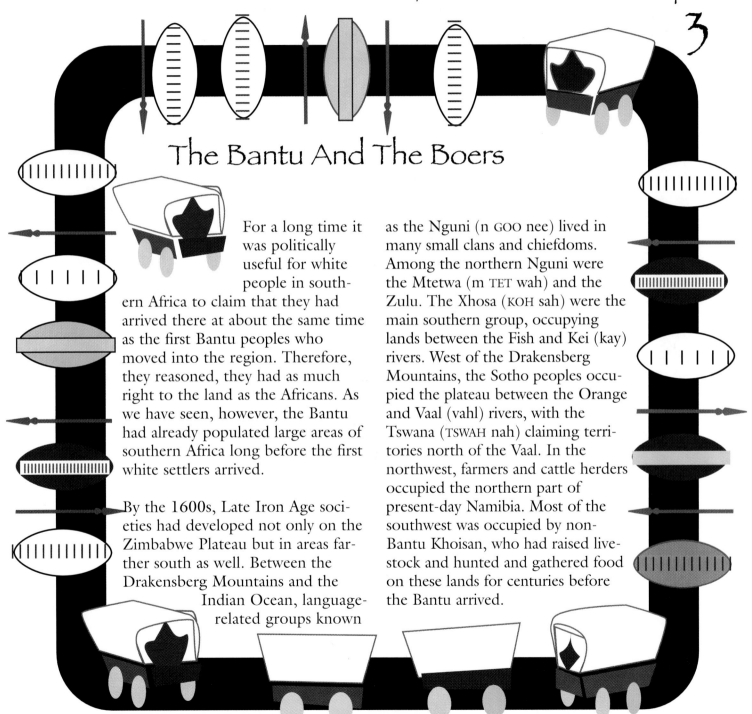

The Bantu And The Boers

For a long time it was politically useful for white people in southern Africa to claim that they had arrived there at about the same time as the first Bantu peoples who moved into the region. Therefore, they reasoned, they had as much right to the land as the Africans. As we have seen, however, the Bantu had already populated large areas of southern Africa long before the first white settlers arrived.

By the 1600s, Late Iron Age societies had developed not only on the Zimbabwe Plateau but in areas farther south as well. Between the Drakensberg Mountains and the Indian Ocean, language-related groups known as the Nguni (n GOO nee) lived in many small clans and chiefdoms. Among the northern Nguni were the Mtetwa (m TET wah) and the Zulu. The Xhosa (KOH sah) were the main southern group, occupying lands between the Fish and Kei (kay) rivers. West of the Drakensberg Mountains, the Sotho peoples occupied the plateau between the Orange and Vaal (vahl) rivers, with the Tswana (TSWAH nah) claiming territories north of the Vaal. In the northwest, farmers and cattle herders occupied the northern part of present-day Namibia. Most of the southwest was occupied by non-Bantu Khoisan, who had raised livestock and hunted and gathered food on these lands for centuries before the Bantu arrived.

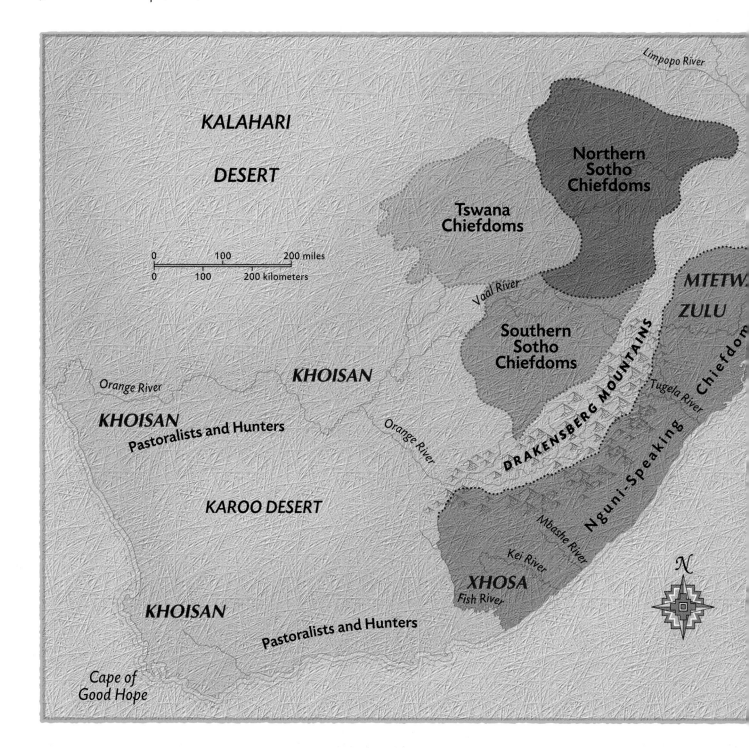

KALAHARI

DESERT

Northern
Sotho
Chiefdoms

Tswana
Chiefdoms

0   100   200 miles
0   100   200 kilometers

Vaal River

Southern
Sotho
Chiefdoms

MTETW
ZULU

Orange River

KHOISAN

Orange River

KHOISAN
Pastoralists and Hunters

DRAKENSBERG MOUNTAINS

Tugela River

Nguni-Speaking Chiefdom

KAROO DESERT

Mbashe River

Kei River

XHOSA
Fish River

KHOISAN

Pastoralists and Hunters

Cape of
Good Hope

N

LATE IRON AGE SOCIETIES
SOUTH OF THE
LIMPOPO RIVER

- Northern Sotho Chiefdoms
- Southern Sotho Chiefdoms
- Tswana Chiefdoms
- Nguni-speaking Chiefdoms

XHOSA Ethnic group

Delagoa Bay

INDIAN OCEAN

Although there was some trade between these different peoples, they were mostly self-sufficient. They did not, however, use sophisticated agricultural techniques to preserve their land. When grazing was not good or the rains failed, when land was used up or clans came into conflict, people simply moved on to new places. For thousands of years there had been enough land for everyone. In the seventeenth century, this was to change forever.

In 1453 the Turks captured the city of Constantinople—the gateway and the trade routes between Europe and the East. From India and China, merchants brought spices, silk, porcelain, and other luxury goods to Europe. When the Turks closed these routes, the Europeans had to find new ways to reach the lucrative eastern markets. They suspected that they might be able to sail around Africa and from there to India and the Far East. After many attempts at this, Vasco da Gama became the first European to succeed. He rounded the Cape of Good Hope in 1498.

New Settlers Arrive

While the Bantu were migrating and settling all over Africa, Europeans too were seeking to expand their territories and find new opportunities for trade. During the fifteenth century, Prince Henry "the Navigator" of Portugal financed many journeys of exploration south along the west African coast. By the 1470s the Portuguese had established trading relations with West Africa. By the early sixteenth century, they had settled in the old kingdoms of Kongo and Ndongo (n DON goh), in present-day Angola. And by 1505 they had built their forts at Sofala and Mozambique on the east coast.

Elsewhere on the continent, trade, not settlement, had usually been the basis of early meetings between Africans, Arabs, and Europeans. Foreign traders on African soil treated Africans as equals and respected their laws and customs. In southern Africa, however, most Europeans came primarily to settle. Their claims on land caused conflicts that have not yet been resolved.

By the sixteenth century, not only the Portuguese but also the Dutch and the British were making regular voyages around the southern tip of Africa to trade in India, southeast Asia, and Indonesia. The Cape of Good Hope was the halfway point on this long journey. By the seventeenth century, Table Bay—so-called because of its flat-topped mountain visible from the sea—had become a regular port of call on the voyage from Europe to Asia. There, ships could stop for repairs while their crews replenished their fresh water supplies and bought cattle, sheep, goats, and milk from local Khoisan herders.

At first, the Khoisan were happy to oblige. Previously they had traveled the long overland route to the Xhosa on the east coast to trade their meat

In this painting, Vasco da Gama confronts the Phantom of the Cape of Good Hope. In 1488, Bartholomeu Dias was the first European to reach the Cape. He named it the Cape of Storms. But the king of Portugal, who hoped that his sailors would reach Asia, renamed it the Cape of Good Hope. ▶

for iron, copper, and beads. Now they could easily obtain these goods from passing ships. The Khoisan, however, were the only meat suppliers in the area and demanded large quantities of trade goods for their meat. Moreover, they would sell only their surplus livestock. This soon led to conflict. The Europeans needed more meat at lower prices, and so European sailors began to raid Khoisan settlements, escaping on their ships with the livestock. The Khoisan retaliated against sailors on the next ships coming in. The food supply at the Cape thus became too expensive and unreliable for European traders.

To solve these problems, the Dutch East India Company, which held a monopoly on trade with the Far East, decided to form a permanent settlement at the Cape. In 1652, the com-

Khoisan traders brought goats, sheep, and cattle for trade with Europeans at Table Bay. They received iron, copper, and beads in exchange. ▼

Reading the Bible was a daily ritual in Boer homes. The Boers, or Afrikaners, led a strict, Protestant way of life. They believed that Africans were the biblical "children of Ham," chosen by God to be the whites' slaves forever. These racist ideas formed the foundation of South Africa's policy of *apartheid* (uh PAHR tayt).

pany built a fort there, as well as a hospital for sick sailors. It developed a large fruit and vegetable garden and paid agents to act as go-betweens in trade with the Khoisan. But this scheme floundered. The gardens could not supply enough food for passing ships. And the Europeans failed to understand that, by taking cattle from the Khoisan, they were removing the very foundation of Khoisan livelihood and culture. In return, the Europeans gave only copper, beads, tobacco, and alcohol—all insignificant items—to the Khoisan. The Europeans would not trade iron or guns for fear of Khoisan attack.

In 1657 the Dutch East India Company attempted to create a reliable food supply at the Cape by allowing some soldiers to settle on permanent farms in the Table Bay area. The company provided these settlers, called Boers (BOH urz)—Dutch for "farmers"— with slave labor from West Africa. The farmers produced fruit and vegetables, which were sold at a profit to passing ships, along with captured Khoisan livestock. In effect, the settlement at Table Bay had developed into a small export trading community.

The Boer farms were, of course, located on Khoisan land, which sometimes appeared "unused" because the Khoisan moved their cattle away to seasonal grazing grounds. Traditionally the Khoisan had survived in the dry regions of the southwest by living in

Vasco da Gama and others had voyaged to Africa to find spices, to discover new routes to the Orient, and to convert Africans to Christianity. They had not planned to trade in slaves. But very soon after Christopher Columbus made his first voyage to the Americas in 1492, Europeans there developed silver mines and huge sugar and tobacco plantations. These needed thousands of laborers. Slavery was a common practice both in Europe and in Africa at the time. So it seemed logical to the Europeans to buy Africans as laborers. By the late eighteenth century, when the trade reached its peak, millions of Africans had been transported across the Atlantic. For economic reasons, as well as because of the growth of the anti-slavery movement, slavery was abolished by the British in 1807.

small groups. They had had no reason to form organized states. But now, with their very survival threatened, their many small clans united and actually forced the Boers back to their fort at the Cape. But the Khoisan were unable to take the fort. Khoisan leaders who met with the Dutch Company commander were told that they had "lost" the war and therefore their lands, which now "belonged" to Dutch settlers.

From this point on, rapid northward and eastward expansion by Dutch farmers onto Khoisan lands was inevitable. Cattle raids deep into the interior increased, draining the region of its livestock and robbing the Khoisan of their age-old way of life. They were easily defeated. Some joined the Boers or remained on their farms as unpaid workers. Others retreated far to the north, while some continued resistance in the form of sporadic guerrilla warfare.

In the meantime the Dutch East India Company had encouraged immigration. By the 1700s, there were a thousand Europeans settled at Table Bay and in the fertile valleys nearby. Using slave labor imported from Mozambique, Madagascar, and Indonesia, they grew wheat, vegetables, and fruit, especially grapes for wine. A cen-tury later, the white population of 21,000 was far outnumbered by the slave popula-tion. In the nineteenth century, whites began referring to the servile class of Dutch-speaking Khoisan, freed slaves, and Afro-Europeans of mixed blood as "Cape Colored." These people were not just dis-possessed of their lands and their freedom; along with all blacks, they were also refused full rights of citizenship in most of the nations later created by Europeans in southern Africa.

Trekboers in the Interior

The wealthier Dutch farmers paid the East India Company rent for their land and remained on their farms. But less wealthy immigrants who could not afford to do so adopted a pastoral way of life much like that of the indigenous peoples of southern Africa. They claimed vast areas of land where the hunting and grazing were good. When these lands were used up, they moved on to other areas, which they added to their hold-ings. Known as *trekboers* from the Dutch word *trek*, meaning "to pull," they traveled thousands of miles across the country in long trains of ox-drawn wagons.

The *trekboers* had very large families. When each son came to adulthood at age 16, he

▲ Boer men were tough individuals who roamed the African bush in search of new pastures for their livestock. They were always well armed and ready for combat, either with Africans or with the British.

Veld: a Dutch word meaning "plain." The highveld is the area of high-altitude plateaus in the southeast. The lowveld is the arid plains of the southwest and central regions.

too laid claim to a huge "farm," stocked with sheep and cattle raided from Khoisan rivals. In this way, *trekboer* expansion to the north and east proceeded very rapidly. By 1760, one group had crossed the Orange River. By the 1770s, another group had reached fertile grazing lands known as the Zuurveld (ZOOR felt), west of the Fish River.

Meanwhile, the Nguni peoples of the east coast had been undergoing momentous changes. Until the eighteenth century, they had lived relatively peacefully along the eastern seaboard, between the Gamtoos and Tugela rivers. Traditionally, these groups raised cattle and grew crops such as sorghum, millet, beans, and pumpkins. Portuguese settlers, however, who had settled at

Sofala, Mozambique, and Delagoa Bay on the east coast, had introduced maize from the Americas into the region. In the last half of the eighteenth century, unusually high rainfall produced bumper crops of maize, resulting in surplus food and thus a sudden increase in population. More land was cleared and cultivated, and cattle herds grew larger. At the same time, trade between the northern Nguni and the Portuguese at Delagoa Bay flourished. The most valued export item there was ivory, and there was intense competition for the elephant-rich hunting grounds of the coastal belt.

The Nguni took advantage of their new-found prosperity to gain more land for their increased population. Under the brilliant leadership of their king, Dingiswayo (dihn gihs WAY oh), the Mtetwa began to conquer smaller groups such as the Zulu and to expand their territory in all directions. Meanwhile, the southern Xhosa were expanding westward into the Zuurveld, which provided them with essential summer grazing grounds. They found little resistance among the Khoisan, who were simply absorbed into Xhosa life. But with the eastward-expanding *trekboers,* the Xhosa met their match.

At first the Xhosa were able to graze their herds on the unused portions of Boer farms. But before long, as more and more whites settled in the area, serious conflicts arose over grazing rights and cattle raids. Although the Boers had guns and horses, they had no standing army and were torn between tending their farms for vital food supplies and organizing military patrols to control the Xhosa. The Xhosa, however, opposed the Boers with a large, united, and well-organized military front. In 1779 the first of a series of violent frontier wars broke out, in which the eastern Khoisan joined the Xhosa against the Boers.

At this time, the picture became even more complicated. By now, the British had become a major world power abroad and were building a vast international trade network. They needed a supply station at the Cape for ships sailing to India. They also needed a naval base to protect their ships from attack by rival European powers. In 1806 the British took over the Dutch East India Company and the Cape Colony.

The Boers traveled thousands of miles in covered ox-drawn wagons.

There was now nothing to stop the efficient British army and determined English farmers from colonizing the entire region. Their forces were far superior to those of the Boers or any African group. A strong British military force came to the aid of the beleaguered Boers in the Zuurveld. The Xhosa put up fierce resistance, but in 1835 the British finally annexed Xhosa territory. The Boers expected that this region would now be opened to white settlement. But in a surprising reverse move, the British declared that maintaining its security would be too expensive, and the region was handed back to the jubilant Xhosa.

During this period the slave trade was grinding to a halt. The Boers, however, felt that Africans were "destined" to be the whites' slaves forever and so treated their black workers and servants with abominable cruelty. The British in southern Africa tried to force the Boers to change these practices. In disgust, the Boers packed up and headed north in search of new lands, far from British control.

This Boer migration, which took place in the 1830s and 1840s, came to be

"I myself have been an eyewitness of Boers coming to a village and . . . demanding twenty or thirty women to weed their gardens, and have seen these women . . . carrying their food on their heads, their children on their backs, and instruments of labor on their shoulders. Every one of

known as the Great Trek. It has been glorified by historians as the beginning of the Afrikaner nation in South Africa. It was, in fact, not an organized event under one leader, but simply the northern migration of many small groups searching for new, secure lands that they could call their own. Wherever the Boers went, they met with African resistance. They could only settle where they were able to overcome hostile African nations, and it was not until the 1840s and 1850s that they were able to claim Orange Free State, between the Orange and Vaal rivers, and Transvaal, between the Vaal and the Limpopo rivers, as their own.

The Boers' troubles were not yet over, however. The future was to bring further unsettling changes and even greater conflicts with the British. The question now was, Who would dominate South Africa—the Africans, the Boers, or the British? It would take another 150 years of warfare and negotiation to settle the question once and for all.

the Boers . . . lauded his own humanity and justice . . . : 'We make the people work for us in consideration of allowing them to live in our country.'"
—*David Livingstone, 1840s*

◀ In 1840 the Boers fought the Zulu and annexed their territory. The Boers drew their wagons into a circle and filled the spaces between the wheels with thornbushes. This gave them a strong position from which to fight the fierce Zulu army.

◄African, Boer,
British, and other
settlers found plenty
of game to hunt
in the wide savannahs
of southern Africa.
Elephants were
much in demand for
their ivory.

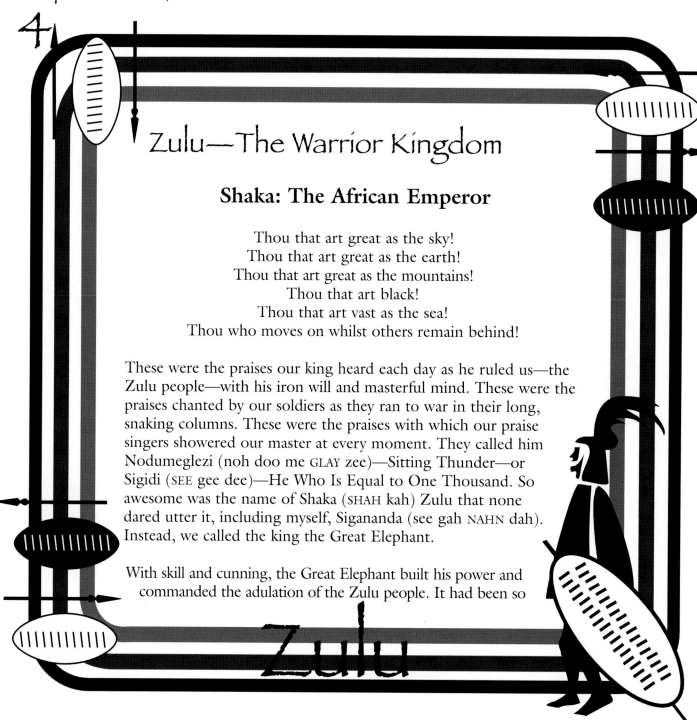

Zulu—The Warrior Kingdom

Shaka: The African Emperor

Thou that art great as the sky!
Thou that art great as the earth!
Thou that art great as the mountains!
Thou that art black!
Thou that art vast as the sea!
Thou who moves on whilst others remain behind!

These were the praises our king heard each day as he ruled us—the Zulu people—with his iron will and masterful mind. These were the praises chanted by our soldiers as they ran to war in their long, snaking columns. These were the praises with which our praise singers showered our master at every moment. They called him Nodumeglezi (noh doo me GLAY zee)—Sitting Thunder—or Sigidi (SEE gee dee)—He Who Is Equal to One Thousand. So awesome was the name of Shaka (SHAH kah) Zulu that none dared utter it, including myself, Sigananda (see gah NAHN dah). Instead, we called the king the Great Elephant.

With skill and cunning, the Great Elephant built his power and commanded the adulation of the Zulu people. It had been so

Zulu

from the very first day of his reign. For on this day, though I was but a boy, I recall how he entered his father's kraal from whence he had been banished for many long years. During those years, the Great Elephant had fought for Dingiswayo, king of the Mtetwa. Through his unparalleled bravery and skill as a warrior he had become commander of the fearless *Izi-cwe* (ee ZEE kwe) regiment. Now he was returning to claim his rightful heritage—the Zulu throne. And I was present when a high-ranking commander assembled our headmen and told them: "Children of Zulu! Today I present to you Shaka, son of Senzangakona (sen zahn gah KOH nah), son of Jama (JAH mah), descended from Zulu, as your lawful chief. Is there any person here who contests the righteousness of this decision? If so, let him stand forth and speak now, or hereafter be silent."

Though there were others with claims to the throne, no one dared to object, for we greatly feared the magnificent Mtetwa warriors. They stood behind the king, resplendent in their kilts and feathers, proudly carrying their spears, their tall shields, and their short stabbing *assegais* (ah SE gyz). We knew that they were trained to kill on command and would not hesitate to use their weapons. And on that first day, I witnessed how the new king ordered the execution of his former enemies—all those whose cruelty to him in his youth he had never forgotten; and all those who did not sufficiently raise their voices in joy at his succession. It was on this day that the new king selected me, Sigananda, to be his servant in war, to carry his mat and his weapons and to attend to his needs.

At once, the Great Elephant began to build his army. For we Zulus were few in number. We had no army, and ours was but a small territory.

First, the king called to him all our men who could fight—from the youngest to the oldest—and formed them into regiments that we called

> **Kraal:** an Afrikaans word meaning "enclosed village"; similar to a corral. (Afrikaans is a version of the Dutch language spoken by Dutch settlers in Africa, who were known as Afrikaners.)
>
> **Assegai:** a spear.

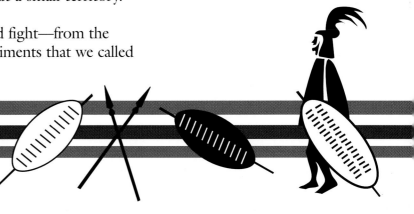

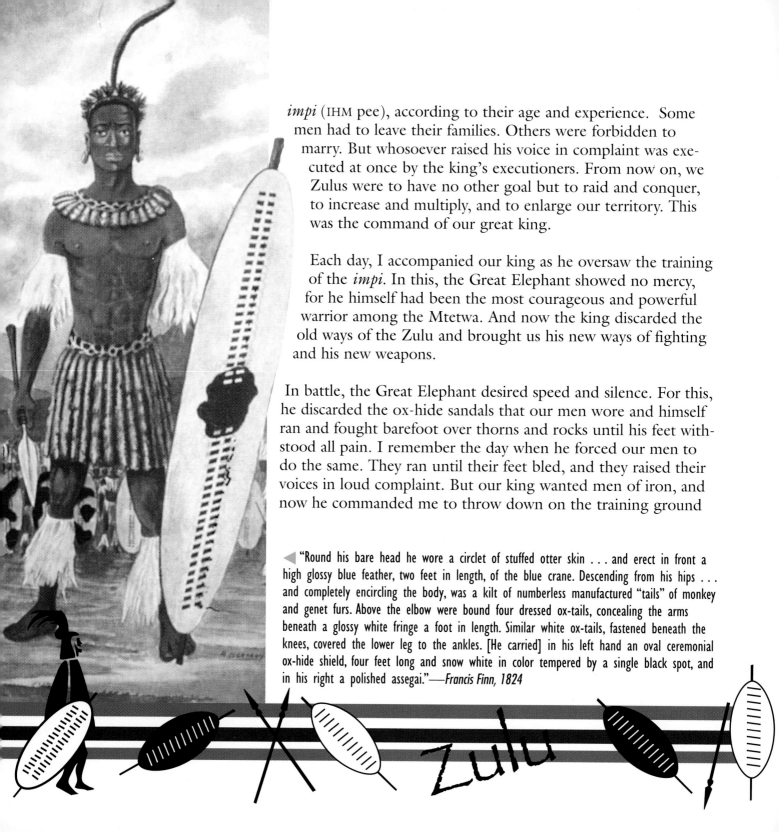

impi (IHM pee), according to their age and experience. Some men had to leave their families. Others were forbidden to marry. But whosoever raised his voice in complaint was executed at once by the king's executioners. From now on, we Zulus were to have no other goal but to raid and conquer, to increase and multiply, and to enlarge our territory. This was the command of our great king.

Each day, I accompanied our king as he oversaw the training of the *impi*. In this, the Great Elephant showed no mercy, for he himself had been the most courageous and powerful warrior among the Mtetwa. And now the king discarded the old ways of the Zulu and brought us his new ways of fighting and his new weapons.

In battle, the Great Elephant desired speed and silence. For this, he discarded the ox-hide sandals that our men wore and himself ran and fought barefoot over thorns and rocks until his feet withstood all pain. I remember the day when he forced our men to do the same. They ran until their feet bled, and they raised their voices in loud complaint. But our king wanted men of iron, and now he commanded me to throw down on the training ground

◄ "Round his bare head he wore a circlet of stuffed otter skin . . . and erect in front a high glossy blue feather, two feet in length, of the blue crane. Descending from his hips . . . and completely encircling the body, was a kilt of numberless manufactured "tails" of monkey and genet furs. Above the elbow were bound four dressed ox-tails, concealing the arms beneath a glossy white fringe a foot in length. Similar white ox-tails, fastened beneath the knees, covered the lower leg to the ankles. [He carried] in his left hand an oval ceremonial ox-hide shield, four feet long and snow white in color tempered by a single black spot, and in his right a polished assegai."—*Francis Finn, 1824*

Zulu

many branches of the four-spiked devil-thorn. On this, our warriors had to run and stamp their feet until they too were hardened to pain. And this they willingly did, for death was the punishment for those who wept or lamented their lot. And in this way was our army built, of men who knew no fear, who scorned pain, and who would die for their king.

Before the coming of the Great Elephant, our Zulu warriors had made many cattle raids. They hurled their spears at their rivals, taunting them with threats and insults. Then they rushed into battle, shields at the ready, each man for himself. But now, in the great battles for our kingdom, the Great Elephant demanded silence so that the warriors could better hear their leaders' commands. No longer did they advance in wild mobs; but the king formed them into the head, horns, and chest of the mighty buffalo. The warriors of the "head" approached the enemy steadfastly, swords at the ready. The "horns" branched to outflank the enemy on each side. Behind the "head" waited the warriors of the "chest," silent, hidden by the shields of the foremost ranks, ready to attack on command.

Our king himself carried a short, wide blade that dealt certain death in hand-to-hand combat. This blade was made by the great wizard Ngonyama (n goh NYAH mah). His forge was greatly feared because it was said that he greased his deadly blades with human fat. Yet, for the Great Elephant, Ngonyama prepared a consecrated blade, endowed with magical properties. And with each deadly thrust of this sword, the king cried: "*Ngadla!*" (n GAHD lah)—"I have eaten!"—as his enemy fell lifeless to the ground.

Our great leader took all the spears of the Zulu men to the ironsmiths, commanding them to fashion from the metal these new, short blades. And he taught our *impi* to kill as he did, to aim for the very belly and heart of the foe. No longer did each warrior enter the fray at will, but the Zulu army fought as one man, one head, one heart.

Zulu

As he built his army, so did the Great Elephant build his royal kraal, where I dwelled for many years. In the center was the great cattle pen. Here, the king liked to observe his vast herd whose every name and markings he knew instantly. And here, he paraded his regiments and held his court. A multitude of huts surrounded this central arena, and beyond these a great wooden palisade protected us from marauders and wild beasts. This great kraal our king named Bulawayo (boo lah WAY oh)—"the Place of Killing"— and thus we, his people, came to know his intentions.

I became accustomed to the many deaths each day that our king inflicted upon us. But what happened next fills me with fear and trembling to this day. There had been at one time many evil omens that boded ill for the king. We had heard a crow speaking with human words and had seen a porcupine—that harbinger of all that is dark—enter into the kraal. Lightning struck at two cows, scorching their hearts, and a heron flew each day over our huts.

Evildoers had caused these signs, and our king knew that they must be immediately found and destroyed. Thus the Great Elephant summoned Nobela (noh BE lah), the leader of our witch-hunters, whose duty it is to smell out these evildoers. And we lived in dread, for whoever was accused by Nobela and her cursed apprentices would die, as would all the members of their kraal.

Our men were summoned to attend, and for three days they came to Bulawayo from every distant kraal. On the appointed day, they gathered in silent dread before our king. Though I was but an innocent youth, servant of my master, I knew not whether I would live or die. Perhaps this day was to be my last?

At length, chilling wails like the death cries of the hyena pierced our silence. Led by Nobela in a demon's dance, the witch-hunters entered

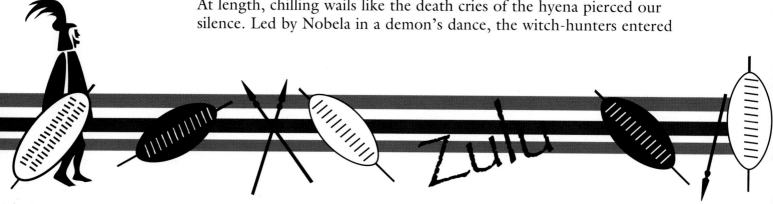

the arena. My knees shook as they moved among us, screaming and wailing. Their faces swam before me, evil black masks streaked with white, on whom no man could easily cast his eye. I saw their writhing bodies, hung with snakeskins and inflated bladders. From their necks swung goats' horns and the teeth and claws of leopards and hyenas, while on their chests grinned the naked skulls of baboons. They spun and twirled, and crawled upon the ground like chameleons, sniffing, smelling out the guilty ones.

In a trance, the men began to chant, for it was the custom with us to guide the witch-hunters toward those whom we thought guilty. And so we chose Sikunyana (see koon YAH nah), for had he not refused Nobela's charms for his fields, yet his maize had grown taller than that of any other man? How could this be? We chanted, louder and louder. All at once, Nobela leaped into the air, sweeping the tail of a wildebeest across Sikunyana's face, and thus condemning him to death. And we saw him taken by the executioners and impaled upon a sharp skewer, where he took many hours to die.

But now, the witch-hunters commenced to single out for death Mgobozo (m goh BOH zoh) and Mdlaka (m duh LAH kah), our king's most trusted commanders. These men the Great Elephant could not kill. Fearless before all-powerful Nobela, he stood forth and commanded her to cease. Zulu warriors would not be denounced! From now on, our king proclaimed, the *impi* and all the generals were to be excluded from the witch-hunters' accusations. This was a great moment, for never before had any Zulu dared to confront Nobela and her kind. "*Indaba ipelile!*" (ihn DAH bah ih pe LEE le) the king thundered. "The affair is closed!" And we, thankful that it was over, sang out in one mighty voice of praise: "*Ba-ye-te! Nkosi!*" (bah ye TE n KOH see)—"So be it, O Great One!"

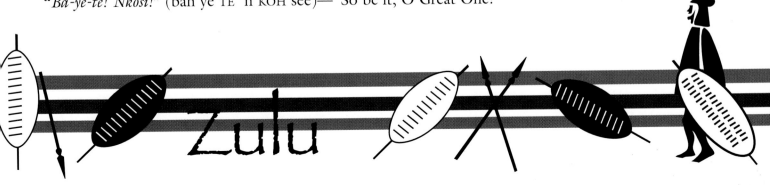

And thus it was with us. Many men were killed that day. Our king spared his warriors but instilled even greater fear among his subjects, for if he could command the witch-hunters, was he not then more powerful than they? Did he then not command their spirit world as well as the natural earth? None dared to speak of this; but in his heart, each one of us knew it to be true.

I am glad that I am now old and was a young man when I served my master, for the Great Elephant took also the authority of the elders and crushed it like the tiny ant under his heel. These were our wise ones whose counsel in all matters we sought and revered. But our king removed them to the status of old women, forcing them to wear many skirts of hide, just as our grandmothers wore. "Do you not see that they impede the king's army?" he sang in his verses. "They were men formerly but they are now our mothers' mothers." We saw and remained silent as our king killed many of our elders, removing with them the last traces of the ancient ways.

The Great Elephant ruled not only the lives of his people. He sought also to command our inner hearts. Thus to mourn the dead of any but the royal household was forbidden. To break this rule meant death, even for the smallest of children. And at his court, the Great Elephant daily wielded his power. Only his executioners knew the secret signs that told them who should live and who should die. And though the condemned had committed no crime, still they sang our king's praises as they went to their deaths. And I, Sigananda, remained silent in the hope that I might live.

In these ways did the king rise to power, almighty and omnipotent, feared and obeyed. And in these ways did the king earn his praise names. We called him Nodumeglezi—Sitting Thunder; and Sigidi—He Who Is Equal to One Thousand. He was the Great Elephant. Now that he is gone to the ancestors, may I dare to say his name? It was Shaka—king of the Zulus.

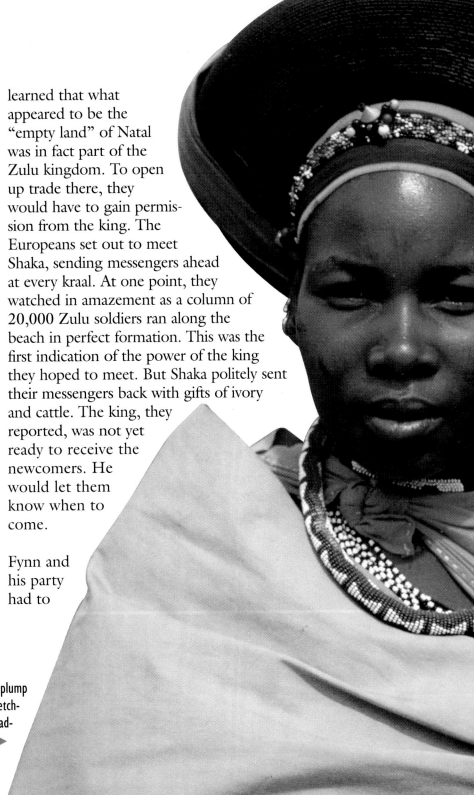

Encounters with Shaka

Early in the twentieth century, the author E. A. Ritter, a South African who spoke fluent Zulu, interviewed many veterans of the Zulu wars to obtain information for his book about Shaka. A vital source for Ritter was Chief Sigananda Cube (KOO be), who had led a Zulu revolt against the British and was captured by them in 1906. He was 96 years old when Ritter interviewed him.

Several Europeans actually witnessed some of the events described by Sigananda. Among them was Henry Francis Fynn, a 30-year-old English adventurer who had learned some of the Bantu languages and was trying to open up the area south of the Zulu heartland for trade. Another was Frances George Farewell, survivor of a shipwreck on the Natal coast and leader of the effort to found a settlement there. These two and a few others were to become the founders of Port Natal, later renamed Durban.

Fynn and Farewell arrived in Natal in July 1824. From a nearby clan in hiding from Shaka's warriors, the Europeans learned that what appeared to be the "empty land" of Natal was in fact part of the Zulu kingdom. To open up trade there, they would have to gain permission from the king. The Europeans set out to meet Shaka, sending messengers ahead at every kraal. At one point, they watched in amazement as a column of 20,000 Zulu soldiers ran along the beach in perfect formation. This was the first indication of the power of the king they hoped to meet. But Shaka politely sent their messengers back with gifts of ivory and cattle. The king, they reported, was not yet ready to receive the newcomers. He would let them know when to come.

Fynn and his party had to

Zulu girls are considered beautiful when they are plump and healthy. The elaborate headdress is made by stretching the hair over a light, wooden frame. Special headrests protect the style during sleep. ▶

▲ Young Zulu dancers prepare for a performance. Their dances often depict the colonial takeover of the ancient kingdom. Here they are in the traditional garb of warriors.

return to Port Natal to await the king's pleasure. Meanwhile, Shaka had sent spies to follow the strangers. When the spies reported that there was much to be learned from the Europeans, Shaka invited them to Bulawayo, where they were to be frequent visitors. Until then, the Europeans had experienced only the meager settlements of the wandering Khoi people near the Cape. As they passed through Zululand, however, they were astonished to find large, orderly kraals and well-tended fields. Clearly these were a wealthy, highly organized people who would have to be met on their own terms.

The Europeans saw Shaka at the height of his power. Indeed, they were lucky to escape alive, for they witnessed daily the terrible killings with which Shaka demonstrated his authority. For his part, Shaka had no intention of executing the Europeans. He was eager to learn from

Many European ships foundered off the coast of Natal. A few survivors were rescued by other ships, but most died or simply merged into African life. In 1683, some British survivors of a wreck reported meeting a Portuguese man who had been wrecked 42 years earlier. He was living happily among the Mpondo (m PON doh) with his African wife and children and had "forgotten everything, his God included."

Jakot Msimbiti (m seem BEE tee) was a Xhosa cattle thief captured by the British. Because he spoke several Bantu languages and some Dutch and English, he was used as an interpreter. In 1823 he capsized with Frances George Farewell in a small boat while exploring the Natal coast. An excellent swimmer, Msimbiti saved Farewell from drowning. Another survivor accused him of deliberately upsetting the boat, at which he ran off into the interior. At Bulawayo, the Europeans were astonished to recognize Msimbiti. He had been renamed Hlabamanzi (hlah bah MAHN zee), "the swimmer," and had been appointed by Shaka to the post of court interpreter.

Shaka's kraal, named Bulawayo, had a central arena of more than a square mile. It was here that his regiments drilled for war and the witch-hunters performed their "smelling out" ceremonies. The central arena was surrounded by about 1,000 huts encircled by a high wooden fence. In a similar kraal, Shaka kept his cattle, which Francis Fynn counted to number over 5,000. ▼

them, to impress them with his huge wealth and military prowess, and to use them when it suited him.

In 1825, 17-year-old Nathaniel Isaacs arrived in Natal to join Farewell's trading company. He was to become Shaka's closest European associate and faithfully recorded everything he witnessed among the Zulus. Once the Europeans had established contact with Shaka and had demonstrated the killing power of their muskets, they were required—often against their will—to accompany the king on several of his raids.

The European reports clearly indicate both the admiration and the horror with which the Europeans regarded the king. When they first entered the kraal at Bulawayo, they found themselves in the midst of a huge crowd of warriors. Fynn recognized Shaka by his superb physique and royal bearing and described how he suddenly "raised a stick in his hand and after striking it right and left and springing out from amidst the chiefs, the whole mass broke from their position and formed up into regiments. Portions of these rushed to the river and the surrounding hills,

while the remainder, forming themselves into a circle, commenced dancing with Shaka in their midst. It was a most exciting scene, surprising to us, who could not have imagined that a nation termed 'savages' could be so well disciplined." Between 8,000 and 10,000 girls, organized into female regiments, also joined in the festivities.

After this initial excitement, however, Fynn's reports become more sober: "On the first day of our visit we had seen no less than ten men carried off to death. On a mere sign by Shaka, the pointing of his finger, the victim would be seized by his nearest neighbors: his neck would be twisted, and his head and body beaten with sticks. . . . Their bodies were then carried to an adjoining hill and there impaled." On another occasion, Fynn reported seeing "60 boys under 12 years of age dispatched [executed] before he [Shaka] had breakfasted."

What was the reason for this systematic terrorization of Shaka's own people? He is quoted as saying that

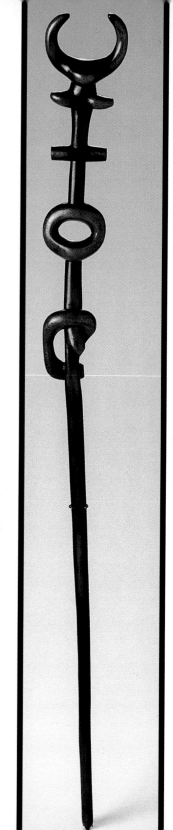

This chief's staff was made in the nineteenth century as a form of tribute to Shaka Zulu. It is topped with the horns and ears of a cow. A snake coils around the center. ▶

This lidded vessel was carved from a single piece of wood by a northern Nguni craftsman in the late nineteenth century. It may have been commissioned as a status symbol for a chief. ▶

"the Zulu people were unruly and understood nothing but cruelty." Was Shaka insane, a man without morals, driven by inhuman desires? Or was he a brilliant though ruthless tyrant who understood that only with total power could he forge a true Zulu nation? Historians have no cut-and-dried answers to these questions. But some have reached back to Shaka's childhood to find clues to the man's character.

The Outcast

Until Shaka's rise to power, the Zulus had been a tiny clan of perhaps 1,500 people living in an area of about 260 sq km (100 sq mi). There were perhaps 500 men capable of fighting. Farther to the north was the territory of the far more powerful Mtetwa.

The Mtetwa were beginning to expand their territories. Their king, Dingiswayo, thus developed his army to an

One eyewitness described traditional warfare in southern Africa as follows: "A day having been mutually arranged beforehand, each clan turned out *en masse* to enjoy the excitement. A core or two of warrior youths bearing *assegais* and shields marched proudly and gleefully forth, with as many women and girls to stand behind and cheer.... Each party, drawn up at a distance from the other ... would send forth its chosen braves to single combat in the arena. Such a champion falling wounded would become the prize of the victors and be taken home by them to be ransomed, perhaps before sundown, with a head of cattle.... Over the slain, mutual condolences would be exchanged."
—*Rev. A. T. Bryant, 1929*

extent rare among the Bantu and went to war against his neighbors. Dingiswayo was unusual, however, for he genuinely sought to create peace among these constantly fighting peoples by subduing them and uniting them under his own rule. Dingiswayo was a skilled politician and did manage to suppress about 40 rival Bantu groups. Those who resisted were savagely crushed. But once their loyalty was established, defeated clans were left in peace and allowed to keep their land and cattle. Their chiefs could continue to rule their people as they had always done; they had only to supply the king with a number of young, unmarried warriors for the Mtetwa army.

In this way, Dingiswayo's army grew to number many thousands of men. They fought in regiments according to age, and all were treated equally, no matter where they came from or what their lineage might be. This system cut right through local clan loyalties and attracted young men from several regions, for if they fought with skill and bravery, they could achieve fame and fortune. One of the men called to service under Dingiswayo was the young Zulu known as Shaka.

Shaka's life had been troubled from the start. He was the son of Senzangakona, a Zulu chief, and Nandi, the beautiful but willful daughter of the chief of the nearby Langeni (lahn GE nee). Nguni kinship rules forbade marriage or sexual relations between two such closely related clans; so Shaka was in effect illegitimate. Even before he was born, the Zulu elders referred to the child as *I-Shaka*—"the parasite." And with this cross to bear, the baby Shaka and his mother Nandi were reluctantly given a hut inside Senzangakona's kraal.

Shaka's early years were lonely and unhappy. His father ignored him and his mother. He was puny, unpopular, and constantly ridiculed by the other boys. When Shaka was six and tending the livestock, a dog killed one of his father's sheep. This was reason enough for Senzangakona to banish Shaka and his mother from his kraal.

Nandi took her son and a young daughter back to her people, the Langeni, but she was not welcome there, either. Her affair with Senzangakona had disgraced the clan. Moreover, she was headstrong and difficult. With her two children, she represented nothing more than extra mouths

Zulu huts are built of poles and thickly woven grass just as they were in Shaka's time. ▶

to feed. When a terrible famine struck, the family was once again forced to move. It was no wonder that Shaka developed an intense hatred of the Langeni and took merciless revenge on them when he became king.

For a time, Nandi and her family stayed at her aunt's kraal, under the protection of a man called Mbiya (m BEE yah). Apparently there followed several reasonably happy years for Shaka, who fondly regarded Mbiya as a foster father. During these years, Shaka's physique changed. Taller than most Bantu, he grew to a height of nearly 2 m (over 6 ft) and developed a huge muscular frame. He became an expert with the light throwing spear and was soon looked upon as a leader. Both the Zulu and the Langeni—who had previously scorned and abandoned Shaka—now wanted him for their armies. But it was the Mtetwa king, Dingiswayo, who saw in the young man the promise of not only a great warrior but also a great king.

At the age of 23, Shaka, along with his age-mates, was called up to join Dingiswayo's *Izi-cwe* regiment. He served for six years, eventually becoming the regiment's commander. It was also during this time that Shaka developed the new fighting techniques, described by Sigananda, that were later to make his warriors the scourge of southeastern Africa.

Meanwhile, Senzangakona, Shaka's father and the Zulu chief, was aging. Dingiswayo now ruled over the Zulu, and he suggested to Senzangakona that his own son, Shaka, whom he had so thoroughly rejected, would make an excellent king. Senzangakona apparently agreed but shortly before his death in 1816 he appointed another son, Sigujana (see goo JAH nah), to the throne. Shaka was outraged at this treachery. He sent his half brother, Ngwadi (n GWAH dee), to Sigujana with a brief message: Abdicate or suffer the consequences. Ngwadi now took matters into his own hands and killed Sigujana. Immediately afterwards, Shaka arrived at his father's kraal with the *Izi-cwe* regiment and claimed the throne. In this way, Shaka, eldest son of the Zulu chief, became king.

MFECANE

The Time of Troubles

In the closing years of the eighteenth century, the period of good rainfall in the Nguni territories came to an end. It was followed by a period of terrible famine, called *madlatule*, (mah dlah TOO le), or "eat what you can and say nothing." The drought brought the expansion of the previous years to an abrupt halt. Now there was a desperate struggle for survival as people fought for control over basic resources.

As with all the Bantu peoples, it was the custom among the Nguni for boys and men to be organized into age groups. The youngest boys did the vital work of herding the livestock; the young unmarried men became warriors; and the older married men became elders. During the *madlatule* famine, however, regiments of all ages were used mainly for military purposes as their starving neighbors raided their lands for food.

The competition forced individual clan leaders to give up their own authority and seek the protection of the stronger chiefdoms. Leadership thus became centralized under powerful kings. In the resulting shake-up, the Mtetwa emerged as a major force in the northern Nguni territories.

The Zulu were at this time still a minor group in the Mtetwa kingdom, but between 1816 and 1819 they became involved in

intensive warfare. In fierce battles between the Mtetwa and the Ndwande (n DWAHN de), a northern Nguni clan, Dingiswayo was killed and his troops scattered. The Ndwande claimed victory, but now Shaka came into his own, for he drove them far north out of Zululand and took over leadership of the Mtetwa.

Unlike Dingiswayo, who allowed defeated chiefs to continue ruling their people, Shaka replaced these chiefs with his own royal officials. Clans that did not submit to Shaka's

Shaka's system of terror was common to other absolute rulers around the world. The fourteenth-century Muslim conqueror Timur (Tamerlane) held frequent banquets for his officials at which several were publicly executed in a show of power. In the seventeenth century, Ivan IV of Russia, known as Ivan the Terrible, crushed the nobles and demonstrated his power with methods similar to Shaka's. In the twentieth century, the German leader Adolf Hitler ordered the annihilation of the Jews, and many people died or were imprisoned during Stalin's reign of terror in the Soviet Union.

◀ The Drakensberg Mountains formed a formidable barrier to westward expansion by the Mtetwa, Zulu, and other peoples.

ruthless authority were simply wiped out. Everyone—both young and old—was put to service for the king. The women tended his fields, the men his cattle. Male and female regiments, or *impi*, were housed in military kraals dotted all over Zululand, and young men and women remained in service for years before they were allowed to marry.

The witch-hunters, or *isangomas*, like Nobela, were the most powerful and dangerous of Shaka's internal enemies. Although he believed them to be frauds, he did not hesitate to use them to good effect when the need arose. Nor did he hesitate to confront their awesome power with his own, as he demonstrated when he dared to place all Zulu warriors outside their domain.

By means of a cunning trick, Shaka eventually broke the *isangomas'* hold on power entirely, causing most of them to be killed by the very victims they had selected for death. Shaka himself now became the chief *isangoma*, controller of magic and holder of the highest power in the land. The fear that people had felt toward the witch-hunters was now directed toward the king. The king was almost a god, and his orders could not be questioned, only obeyed.

In these ways, Shaka deliberately broke down ancient traditions and clan loyalties. He fought tirelessly to expand his kingdom in all directions. Areas were completely depopulated as people either fled or were driven out by the brutal Zulu warriors.

Some groups headed north, campaigning as far away as Tanzania and Lake Victoria until they eventually settled in southern Mozambique. Others crossed the Drakensberg Mountains and destroyed the Rozvi kingdom of the western Zimbabwe Plateau before settling near Lake Malawi. Yet others conquered rival groups north of the Pongolo River, where they founded the Swazi (SWAH zee) kingdom. In 1821–22, several groups joined together and fled west, raiding the peaceful Sotho-Tswana communities along the valley of the Caledon River.

In a catastrophic chain reaction, one group of displaced people after another destroyed its rivals in the desperate search for food. By the mid-1820s, some 2.5 million starving, homeless people wandered over the eastern and central regions of southern Africa. Neither a single permanent settlement nor a single clan strong enough to withstand the chaos existed. In desperation, people resorted to cannibalism—a practice as foreign and revolting to the Bantu as it is to most other cultures. No one was safe from the unruly mobs who hid in caves and fell upon passersby, littering the hills and valleys with human bones.

The flame ignited by Dingiswayo in the northern Nguni lands and further fueled by Shaka turned into the greatest disruption of life that the continent had ever known. The Nguni called this devastating time of troubles the *mfecane* (m fe KAH ne), or "the crushing." Farther west, the Tswana and Sotho peoples referred to it as the *difaqane* (dih fah KAH ne)—"the scattering." Europeans called it "the wars of calamity." In reality, however, no words could adequately describe the devastation to people, lands, crops, and settlements, or the misery of the forced migrations.

End of an Era

Although Shaka seemed all-powerful, dissent was growing in the Zulu kingdom. He had driven his people too far. Even his faithful warriors were disgruntled, especially when they were kept fighting for months at a time with no break.

Within the royal household itself, a plot was hatched. On September 22, 1828, at the age of 41, Shaka Zulu was assassinated by his own half brothers, helped by his aunt and his personal servant. The great king of the Zulus was buried in a hastily dug, unmarked pit. To this day his remains lie somewhere under Cupper Street in the small town of Stanger, South Africa.

Shaka had not completed what he had set out to do. Over the years, he had questioned his white guests for hours on end and had become fascinated with everything European, though he still insisted on the superiority of the Zulu way of life. Once Shaka had created a kingdom, he intended to repopulate it with selected Nguni peoples. They would live in peace and become prosperous, and, above all, they would receive European education.

As it is, Shaka Zulu is known only for his reign of terror. It lasted only 12 years, but during that brief time, the many different peoples he ruled forgot their hereditary lineages and came to think of themselves as Zulu. This, then, was his legacy. Under Shaka, what had once been a tiny, insignificant Nguni clan grew to number almost a quarter of a million people living in one of the largest and most powerful kingdoms on the African continent.

New Leaders

Out of the chaos of the *mfecane,* a number of strong leaders emerged. They had gathered many followers and found places to settle. Some of them had begun importing guns from European traders at the Cape or

from Natal, and they were able to hold back European settlement for some time.

Some of these leaders had worse reputations than others. For example, the Tlokwa (TLOH kwah) clan, or "people of the wild cat," was led by a terrifying woman named Mantatisi (mahn tah TEE see). This clan had been displaced by another and set off on a wide path of destruction. By 1823, Mantatisi was rampaging across the southern regions with a mob of some 50,000 followers whom historians later dubbed the Mantatee Horde. Every day, the mob moved on; every day, thousands perished. Mantatisi eventually died, and the Horde, led by her son, ravaged the region for another 20 years.

Another, more successful leader was Mzilikazi (m zih lee KAH zee). He was one of Shaka's favorite generals, chief of a clan that had come under Shaka's authority. In

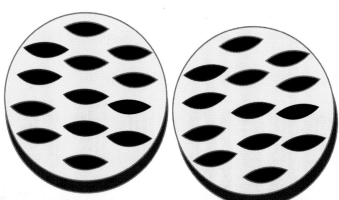

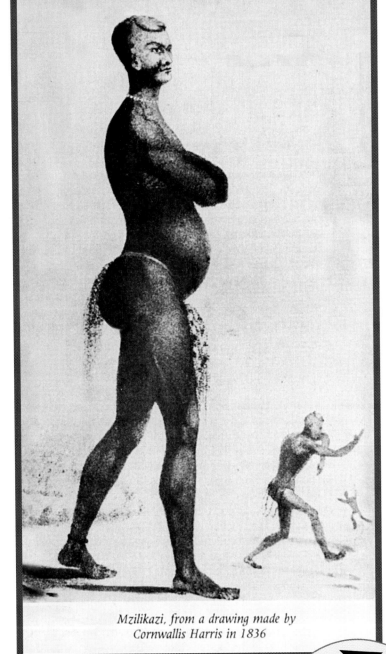

Mzilikazi, from a drawing made by Cornwallis Harris in 1836

◀ The Ndebele king Mzilikazi was a brilliant, ruthless leader. He was also a charming, intelligent man who commanded slavish loyalty from his followers and from those whom he conquered, among them the Sotho, Tswana, and Shona. When he left Zululand, he had only 300 followers. When he died in 1868, aged nearly 80, the Ndebele numbered 150,000.

1822, Mzilikazi was in his early 20s when he deserted Shaka and fled westward with only 300 followers.

Using the military techniques he had learned from Shaka, Mzilikazi led his people to the highveld regions of the Sotho, where he forced thousands of Sotho-Tswana people under his command and soon established his own kingdom. Mzilikazi's followers were the Ndebele (n de BE le), called Matabele (mah tah BE le) by the Sotho. The Ndebele kingdom remained relatively stable for several years.

But Mzilikazi stood in the way of the advancing Boers as they marched northward on their Great Trek. Mounted on horseback and well armed with guns, the Boers soundly defeated the Ndebele in 1838. This time, Mzilikazi led his people north of the Limpopo, where he reestablished his kingdom—later called Matabeleland—among the southern Shona of the Zimbabwe Plateau.

In the western and southwestern regions of southern Africa, people knew nothing of the tumult caused by the *mfecane*. But the pressure of increased populations, expanding states, and European trade and settlement was mounting everywhere. People from the northwest moved south and east, skirting the Kalahari Desert in search of new grazing grounds. North of the Kalahari, clans were being forced south by the expansion of the Lozi state along the Zambezi floodplains. And in the southeast, Xhosa expansion continued to cause conflict between the Boers and the British.

Amidst the turmoil one man stands out above all others—Moshueshue (moh SHWE shwe), leader of the Sotho Mokoteli clan and a survivor of Mantatisi's raids. Showing great diplomacy, intelligence, and tolerance, Moshueshue was able to use the *mfecane* to his own advantage, becoming the sole founder of the kingdom of Basuto. The kingdom was later renamed Lesotho and was ruled for decades by Moshueshue's descendants.

LESOTHO

Lesotho— The Basuto Kingdom

Moshueshue: King of the Mountain

June 28, 1833: Our guide Moseme (moh SE me) was careful to point out to us, not far from the mountain chain and the Caledon River, a greyish point somewhat indistinct in the distance. It was the residence of the chief we were seeking. His mountain was not high, but it had the reputation of being impregnable. It was called Thaba-Bosiu—Mountain of the Night—because, as Moseme explained, it was said to grow much larger when darkness fell.

As to the chief himself, Moseme told us that, having succeeded in making various rivals bow before the rising power of his house, he had taken the name of Moshesh, the "Shaver" or the "Leveler." This superiority, which no one now thought of contesting, he owed to a rare intelligence, to great firmness, and to a skill, quite new in that country, of understanding and managing people.

The Basutos made a most favorable impression upon us. Their skin was soft, bronze rather than black in color, their limbs robust and well modeled. Their average height was the same as our own. We were struck by the

BASUTO

dignity of their bearing, the grace of their movements, and the deference and cordiality which characterized their manner of address.

The hilly character of the country and the absence of roads forcing us to make more than one detour, one of our men was sent in a straight line across country to announce our approach to Moshesh. Along the way, we found on our track terrible indications of massacres and devastations. Almost everywhere were human bones. In some places their number indicated battlefields.

At the foot of a mountain which still concealed Thaba-Bosiu from us, we saw for the first time villages in the level plain. Here everybody was aware of the peaceful nature of our visit. The principal personage respectfully saluted us as the "Foreigners of Moshesh," while he placed at our feet vessels of milk and some baskets of boiled maize.

The moment had come to return to the sovereign of the country the politeness which he had offered to us. Leaving the wagons to continue the journey under the guidance of my companions, I accordingly went forward on horseback with Adam Krotz and his

◀ The missionary Eugene Casalis drew this picture of Moshueshue, king of Basutoland, in 1833 and wrote: "He had allowed to fall carelessly about him . . . a large mantle of panther skins as soft as the finest cloth . . . . For sole ornament he had bound around his forehead a string of glass beads, to which was fastened a tuft of feathers . . . . He wore on his right arm a bracelet of ivory—an emblem of power—and some copper rings on his wrists."

interpreter. In an immense circle formed by the last spurs of the Maluti Range, we soon saw, rising before us, a pentagonal hill completely isolated, which appeared to us to be from 120 to 150 m (400 to 500 ft) high. Its summit was quite flat, and of an area almost equal to that of the base.

This wide and densely populated plain on top of the mountain was completely surrounded by a border of huge perpendicular rocks, which appeared to make access impossible. But as we drew nearer, we saw, at one of the angles of the mountain, a line winding serpentlike around it from the top to the bottom. This was a ravine, serving as a path. By and by we dismounted and, taking our horses by the bridle, climbed as best we could this rugged stairway.

As soon as we showed ourselves at the summit, there was a general rush, everybody wishing to see us first. Suddenly a personage attired in the most fantastic fashion advanced, a long wand in his hand, growling and snapping like a dog. At his appearance everybody retreated and fell into line, making in this way an immense semicircle behind a man seated on a mat. "There is Moshesh," said Krotz to me. The chief bent upon me a look at once majestic and benevolent. His profile, much more noble than that of most of his subjects, his well-developed forehead, the fullness and regularity of his features, his eyes, a little weary, as it seemed, but full of intelligence and softness, made a deep impression on me. I felt at once that I had to do with a superior man, trained to think, to command others, and, above all, to discipline himself.

He appeared to be about 45 years of age. The upper part of his body, entirely naked, was perfectly modeled, sufficiently fleshy, but without obesity. I admired the graceful lines of the shoulders and the fineness of his hand.

After we had looked an instant on each other in silence, he rose and said: *"Lumela lekhoa!"* (loo ME lah le KOH yah)—"Welcome, white

man!" and I replied by holding out my hand to him, which he took without hesitation.

Some days later, having made our camp at the foot of the mountain, we invited Moshesh to dinner and after this repast, the moment came for explaining the object of our arrival. Adam Krotz, speaking first, recalled to the chief the commission he had received from him—that he should bring missionaries to the Basuto people—and said how happy he was to have been able to fulfill it. "Here," he said as he finished, "are the men whom I promised you; it is for them to explain to you their plans and arrange matters with you."

Speaking in our turn, we said how greatly we had been moved by the description which had been given us of the Basutos and of their present sad position. We gave Moshesh to understand that we were the messengers of a God of Peace, whose protection and love were assured us, and who was willing to protect and bless the Basutos also. If Moshesh and his people would consent to place themselves with us under the care and protection of this God, we promised that He would make the enemy attacks cease, and create in the country a new order of belief and of manners which would secure peace, order, and abundance. In order to prove to our new friends the firmness of our convictions, we offered to establish ourselves definitely in their midst, and to share their lot, whatever it might be.

"My heart is white with joy," replied the chief. "Your words are great and good. It is enough for me to see your clothing, your arms, and the rolling houses in which you travel, to understand how much intelligence and strength you have. You see our desolation. This country was full of inhabitants. Wars have devastated it. I remain almost alone on this rock. I have been told that you can help us. You promise to do it. That is enough; it is all I wish to know. Remain with us."

REPUBLIC OF
SOUTH AFRICA

Orange Free State

Natal Province

○ Butha
Buthe

MALUTI MTNS.

DRAKENSBURG MTNS.

Caledon River

⬡ **Maseru**

Thaba Bosiu ▲

Orange River

L E S O T H O

Orange River

East
Cape
Province

Natal
Province

East Cape
Province

REPUBLIC OF
SOUTH AFRICA

LESOTHO ●

Atlantic
Ocean

Indian
Ocean

N

MODERN KINGDOM OF
LESOTHO

⬡ National capital
○ City
▲ Mountain peak

Land over 9000 ft. (2740 m)
6000 - 9000 ft. (1830 - 2740 m)
3000 - 6000 ft. (915 - 1830 m)

0   25   50 miles
0   25   50 kilometers

The Basuto

The Basuto are one of the few peoples in Africa that can trace their origins as a nation to a specific time. It was in 1823 when Moshueshue, called Moshesh by Europeans, became their leader.

Among the first Europeans to meet Moshueshue were three French Presbyterian missionaries of the Paris Evangelical Missionary Society. Their leader was 20-year-old Eugene Casalis, who wrote the preceding report. He and his companions had intended to build a mission farther north, but the area had been ravaged by the Ndebele leader Mzilikazi. The missionaries were at a loss as to their next move when Adam Krotz—a Christian hunter of mixed blood and a friend of Moshueshue's—appeared at their camp. Krotz had persuaded Moshueshue that European mission-aries could act as peacemakers in the conflicts between the Basuto and the Boers. Moshueshue saw the advantages of this idea and asked Krotz to find him some of this strange new breed called "missionary."

The French missionaries were delighted at this turn of events, and accordingly Adam Krotz led them to Moshueshue's stronghold at Thaba-Bosiu. Eventually Casalis built a mission near the mountain, while the other missionaries established one 40 km (25 mi) away. For the next 23 years, Eugene Casalis was Moshueshue's close friend, confidant, and unofficial foreign secretary. The influence of missionaries in Africa has often been criticized, but it is to Casalis and others like him that the Basuto owe their written language, their recorded history, and the preservation of their oral traditions.

At this time the antislavery movement in Europe was in full swing, and the

◀ Eugene Casalis became a close friend of Moshueshue's and mediated between the Basuto king, the Boers, and the British. Other African leaders were also influenced by missionaries. The Ndebele king Mzilikazi befriended the Scottish missionary John Moffat, who advised him to allow Europeans to trade and hunt for ivory in Matabeleland.

missionaries enjoyed solid public support. Politicians, magistrates, and even royalty could not afford to ignore them. Thus Eugene Casalis wielded great power as he took on the important role of mediator in later conflicts between the Basuto, the Boers, and the British.

Mohlomi: The Philosopher

The Caledon River valley forms the western border of present-day Lesotho. Known as the Switzerland of Africa, the country is mountainous, with all of its land rising 1,000 m (3,280 ft) or more above sea level. Great plains stretch between flat-topped hills, and to the east, the Drakensberg Mountains, reaching heights of 3,000 m (9,840 ft) or more, are often capped with snow.

Over 200 million years ago, dinosaurs lived in what is Lesotho today, leaving behind their huge fossilized footprints in the rock. Stone Age people wandered the valleys and plains. Their paintings adorn hundreds of caves. About A.D. 1600, the Basuto people migrated into the region from the north, along with other Bantu groups. Some settled in the Transvaal area, while others lived along the Orange River and its tributaries.

> The people of Basuto speak the Sesuto language and live in Lesotho. A single individual is a Musotho.

The horn of a cow has been hollowed out to form a snuff container with an antelope's head. The Sotho artist used the natural curve of the horn to lend the figure lifelike energy. ▶

▲ One-third of Lesotho is dominated by the thinly populated Maluti Mountains, where it sometimes snows. Most of the towns and villages, the administrative headquarters, and the agricultural land lie on the western plains, between 1,500 and 1,600 m (4,900 and 5, 250 ft) above sea level. Cattle, donkeys, and sheep thrive in these hills.

Before the *mfecane*, the Caledon Valley, located in the center of this vast region, was fairly densely populated by small clans of Basuto. Each clan was headed by a chief, and there were constant cattle raids and minor skirmishes between the groups. No one clan dominated the others, and there was no leader of all the clans.

In 1786 a son was born to Mokachane (moh kah CHAH ne), a member of a minor clan near the upper reaches of the Caledon River. The child was named Lepoqo (le-POH koh), and his intelligence and powerful physique soon distinguished him from the other boys. He was apparently a little wild and unruly and is even said to have killed some comrades. While still in his teens, Lepoqo became a daring cattle raider and attracted a growing number of followers.

When he was about 18, Lepoqo was circumcised with other boys of his age. He then visited the famed chief Mohlomi (moh LOH mee), who lived nearby. Mohlomi was an extraordinary man for his time and culture. He was a wandering philosopher and rainmaker who traveled far and wide, preaching tolerance and peace. Mohlomi blessed Lepoqo by brushing his forehead against his own. He fastened his own long earring—a sign of power—in Lepoqo's ear. The old man then presented Lepoqo with an ox, a shield, and a spear and had a beast slaughtered in his honor.

What had Mohlomi seen in the young man before him? Perhaps it was Lepoqo's willingness to learn and change; perhaps it was his ambition to lead. For years later, Lepoqo, who came to be called Moshueshue, admitted to his son that he had "had a great desire to become a chief" and wanted his power "to grow and overshadow that of others."

Until his death in 1815, Mohlomi was to remain an important influence on Moshueshue. At this first meeting, the young Lepoqo asked Mohlomi what magic or medicine he had used to achieve his status. According to oral reports, Mohlomi answered that "power is not acquired by medicine: the heart is the medicine." He apparently gave Lepoqo further advice: to distrust the witch doctors, whom he believed were wicked frauds; to extend his influence by marrying many women; and to help those in need. At later meetings, Mohlomi prophesied that Lepoqo would lead the Basuto, and advised him to trade with the white-skinned people he had seen on his travels. Mohlomi also dreamed of "a red cloud of dust" on the horizon: a forbidding portent of what was to come.

Lepoqo took Mohlomi's advice to heart. To become a chief, he had to prove that he could provide cattle and food for his people. After one especially daring cattle raid he was renamed Moshueshue. The name was both the word for "razor" and the sound that it makes, and it was appropriate since Lepoqo swept off his rival's cattle, or "shaved their beards." Lepoqo, now known as Moshueshue, married the daughters of neighboring clans and showed himself merciful and wise in his dealings with opponents.

The Basuto trained oxen to lead their cattle when out at pasture and to race riderless over fairly long distances from the pasture to the home kraal. The oxen answered a call, a whistle, or a particular chant and learned to graze near a plumed stick carried by a herder. When the stick was dropped, the race began.

Thaba-Bosiu: The Mountain Fortress

When the wars of 1822–23 broke out, Moshueshue was living in the northern regions of the Caledon. As wave after wave of warring refugees swept the Basuto lands, Moshueshue took his people to a hill called Butha-Buthe (boo THA boo THE), where they were fairly well fortified. But within a year the Tlokwa, led by Mantatisi, were rampaging in the area, which caused Moshueshue to fear for the lives of the Basuto. Again, he moved his entire following, now numbering about 2,000 people. This time, he led them on a perilous journey south to Thaba-Bosiu. Their path led through mountains infested with cannibals who captured and ate Moshueshue's grandfather as he lagged behind.

Moshueshue and his people ascended Thaba-Bosiu at night and were soon settled on its flat top. From this central capital, the Basuto leader began to build his kingdom. Unlike Shaka Zulu's centralized state, the Basuto kingdom was a federation of semi-independent chiefdoms. They had to acknowledge Moshueshue's overall authority, to provide regiments when

▲ Thaba-Bosiu lies about 24 km (15 mi) east of Maseru, Lesotho's capital city, on the Little Caledon River. It is only about 100 m (300 ft) high, yet appears much higher. A sheer rock face surrounds the flat summit of about 60 hectares (150 acres). Of six fissures, or cracks, on this rock face, only three are passable. The Basuto defended their fortress by piling up huge rocks which they rolled down onto their enemies. Thaba-Bosiu was never captured. Deserted except for Moshueshue's grave, it stands today as a fitting monument to the origins of the Kingdom of Lesotho.

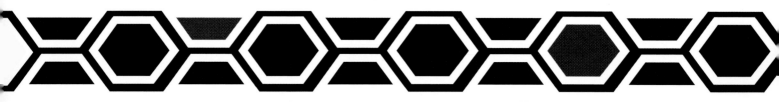

could be grown for his people. He conducted many raids in the region, but the *mfecane* provided him with all the people and cattle he wanted, as thousands of refugees sought and received his protection.

The Basuto army was no match for some of the kingdom's powerful neighbors, so Moshueshue used clever diplomacy rather than warfare. He defeated the Ndebele, but instead of harassing them any further he sent them on their way with a generous gift of cattle. They never attacked him again. Moshueshue also sent cattle as tribute to other rivals and sent furs, girls, and feathers to Shaka, whose Zulu *impi* stayed away from Thaba-Bosiu, although they constantly raided in the region. Moshueshue even supplied some cannibals with cattle. With enough food to eat, they eventually gave up their hideous practice. With successful agriculture, huge herds of cattle, thousands of people under his command, and his impregnable capital, Moshueshue was emerging as one of the most important leaders in southern Africa.

The greatest threat to Moshueshue came from the Afrikaner Boers, who began to appear along the Caledon River in 1831. Soon there were violent conflicts over land. In despair, Moshueshue, aided by Casalis, signed a treaty with the British governor at

required, and to send tribute to the capital. Moshueshue cemented these relationships through a complex system of marriages.

Moshueshue needed every fighting man he could get in order to command large areas of fertile land surrounding Thaba-Bosiu, where food

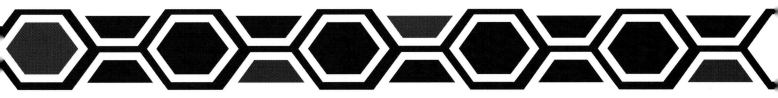

the Cape, making the Basuto allies of the British. But the boundaries of Moshueshue's kingdom were still in question since he claimed lands far to the west, in the Orange Free State, which was occupied by the Boers.

There followed almost 40 years of conflict between the Boers, the British, and the Basuto. Twice, in 1858 and again in 1865, the Boers declared war on the Basuto. During the second war, the Basuto were driven back to their lands east of the Caledon. Thaba-Bosiu itself was besieged, and Moshueshue's people almost starved to death. Moshueshue signed a peace treaty with the Boers, but the violence continued. Finally, at Moshueshue's urgent request, the British stepped in. On March 12, 1866, they annexed Basutoland (as they called the area), proclaiming that "the tribe of the Basutos shall be taken to be for all intents and purposes British subjects, and the territory of the said tribe shall be taken to be British territory." Moshueshue's kingdom was now a British protectorate.

In February 1869 the British signed a boundary treaty with the Boers, who released the Basuto lands east of the Caledon that they had claimed as their own. Moshueshue was disappointed, for with British help he had expected to regain *all* his former territory. Instead the Basuto found themselves crowded into half the area they had previously occupied, on land that could barely support their large numbers of cattle and horses. The borders established then, however, remain today as the boundaries of the present Kingdom of Lesotho.

Moshueshue died on March 11, 1870, at the age of 84. Both Europeans and Africans consider him to have been one of the continent's greatest statesmen. He united desperate refugees in a nation with definite borders and a single language. He held off warring Zulus through diplomacy and prevented the Boers from colonizing Basuto lands by requesting British protection. Moshueshue banned the sale of alcohol and the practice of witchcraft. He set up a system of local councils called *pitsos* that met to make and enforce laws, aided at times by a national *pitso* and overseen by a single supreme chief. This chief distributed land to individuals and clans who used it for farming, but no individual was ever allowed to own land. Most importantly, Moshueshue absolutely forbade and prevented white settlement or land ownership in Basutoland.

It is fitting that when Basuto people return to their homeland today, they say: "I am coming to Moshueshue."

Although he was fascinated by Christianity and spent hours discussing it with Casalis, Moshueshue never converted. When told that one Christian ideal was the abolition of war, he replied: "War is a rod which God has not yet broken." Speaking of various religious orders he had encouraged to found missions among his people, he remarked: "Missionaries are like doctors: one should not always consult the same one."

▲ There is no word for "horse" in Sesuto. The common term is *pere* (PE re), derived from the Dutch word *perd*. The Basuto first obtained horses from the *trekboers*. From Arab sires and English thoroughbreds, breeders at the Cape developed a strong, surefooted horse with amazing endurance. From this stock the Basuto bred a small, immensely strong pony. These ponies soon became, and still remain, a status symbol among Basuto men.

Epilogue

To Europeans at the beginning of the eighteenth century, Africa was *terra incognita*—a land about which they knew very little. Only 100 years later, it had been almost fully mapped, and most of the continent was in the hands of the European powers. In southern Africa as in most other areas, a very small number of Europeans managed to suppress and control millions of Africans. Historians still grapple with the following question: How could the great continent, whose various cultures had survived successfully for centuries, have been so easily overpowered?

The key to European domination of Africa lies in the slave trade. The slave trade began in the early sixteenth century and was immensely profitable to European merchants for the next 200 years. But the costs of purchasing, exporting, and selling slaves were very high. When a surplus in sugar production on American plantations caused sugar prices to drop, profits from the slave trade also dropped dramatically.

In the meantime the Industrial Revolution had transformed Europe. Goods that had previously been made by hand were now mass-produced by machines in factories. Once European demand for these goods had been satisfied, merchants and bankers needed new markets abroad. Africa—the unexplored continent—was the obvious place to go.

During the nineteenth century, declining profits along with the efforts of religious societies and others who opposed slavery finally brought the slave trade to an end. To replace it, Europeans developed the so-called legitimate trade in palm oil, rubber, and other products they had found in Africa. They also dreamed of locating huge unexploited mineral resources hidden in the interior.

From the very start the exploration of Africa had a double purpose: first, to find resources and open up the interior to trade; and second, to convert African "savages" to Christianity. Many explorers in Africa, such as David Livingstone, were missionaries. Others were scientists, former soldiers, or adventurers. They were the first Europeans to make contact with African leaders in the interior and to report on the exploitable resources they found. Livingstone, for example, described bars of copper up to 45 kg (100 pounds) in weight circulating as currency in what is now the Congo.

From the beginning, exploration and colonization went hand in hand. By the mid-nineteenth century in southern Africa, after the initial conflicts over land, the political climate had become more settled. The Boers occupied the Orange Free State, the Transvaal, and smaller areas in the southeast, and the British occupied Cape Colony. Most African groups had settled in their own areas. The Zulu held on to their kingdom in the southeast, Basutoland remained established as a black-ruled nation, the Shona occupied Mashonaland on the eastern Zimbabwe Plateau, and the Ndebele claimed Matabeleland in the western regions of the Plateau. Ivory, ostrich feathers, and animal skins were the main items exported, while guns, manufactured items, and cloth were the main imports. The year 1870, however, was to prove a turning point in southern Africa's history.

While there was turmoil within southern Africa, huge changes were taking place in Europe. Where Britain had once dominated world trade, now other nations were catching up and clamoring for holdings in Africa—called protectorates—where they could monopolize trade. In 1884, representatives of the world powers met at a special conference in Berlin. There they simply divided up the African continent between them, drawing artificial borders as they saw fit. In their "scramble for Africa," the Germans, Belgians, British, French, Italians, Portuguese, and Spanish claimed territories that later became colonies.

Thousands of African and European prospectors flocked to Kimberley when diamonds were discovered there in 1869. When heavy machinery was needed to dig deeper shafts, large mining companies moved in. Cecil Rhodes bought them all out. His check—"Five Million, Three Hundred and Thirty-Eight Thousand, Six Hundred and Fifty-Eight Pounds—Only"—was the largest personal check that had ever been written. ▶

"DIAMONDS, DIAMONDS, DIA-MONDS!" proclaimed the *Natal Mercury* in June 1869. Huge deposits of diamonds had been found near present-day Kimberley in the Boer republics of the Orange Free State and the Transvaal and in neighboring areas claimed by the Griquas (GREE kahz) and other groups. Thousands of speculators, both black and white, converged on the region from all over southern Africa, as well as from the Americas, Australia, and Europe. In 1871, Great Britain hastily annexed Griqualand West, an area to the west of Kimberley. This formed a protective buffer to the richest known diamond-bearing region in the world.

The Europeans completely controlled the mining operations at Kimberley. They had

◄ Cecil John Rhodes was called The Colossus of Africa because of his dream of including the continent "from Cape to Cairo" in the British empire. The British "happen to be the best people in the world," he wrote, "with the highest ideals of decency and justice and liberty and peace, and the more of the world we inhabit, the better it is for humanity." He died of heart disease aged only 49.

the advantages of technology and capital to back their ventures. While some Africans staked their own claims, most were employed as laborers. Eventually, large companies bought out the individual miners. The largest of these, De Beers, was owned by Cecil Rhodes, an English immigrant who had made a fortune in the mines. Rhodes was to play an extremely important role in the history of southern Africa.

The diamond boom had a huge effect on most of southern Africa. At any one time, as many as 50,000 migrant African workers were employed in the mines. They lived in special highly controlled camps away from their families, an arrangement that deliberately disrupted traditional ways of life. Kimberley grew into a bustling town of 30,000 people, and the Boers profited hugely from the increased demands for their agricultural produce.

Inevitably the old conflicts over land rose again. Both the British and the Boers steadily increased white settlement in African-ruled territories. In fact, the British planned to destroy all the remaining kingdoms in the region and to unite all the white-ruled regions into one British federation. It would be financed by profits from the mines and serviced by a huge labor force of former soldiers drafted from the great armies of the Xhosa, Zulu, and other groups. The Africans, however, were better organized and better armed than before, and they offered fierce resistance.

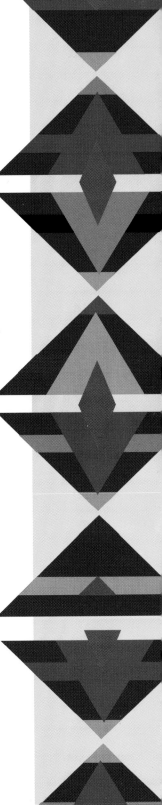

In 1876 the Pedi people of the Transvaal defeated the Boers, almost bankrupting them in the process. In the southeast the British faced such tough opposition from the Xhosa that they gave up trying to seize more Xhosa lands for settlement. And in January 1879 the British confronted their major opponents—the Zulu.

King Cetswayo (setch WAY yoh), who had ruled the Zulu since 1872, launched the full force of his *impi* regiments against the British and enjoyed an astounding initial victory at the battle of Isandhlwana. It took the British eight months and thousands of soldiers before the great Zulu kingdom finally fell to their superior firepower. To reduce Zulu unity, the British divided the kingdom into small artificial states. This fueled local rivalries, which eventually erupted into civil war. A devastating famine struck the final blow. In 1887, with its resistance destroyed, the Zulu kingdom that Shaka had built became a British colony.

The "mineral revolution," which had begun with the diamond boom, continued during this period. In 1886,

huge deposits of gold were discovered in the central Transvaal. Once again, get-rich-quick speculators poured into the region. And once again, the diamond magnate Cecil Rhodes seized control, this time with a powerful mining monopoly called Consolidated Goldfields.

The Boers—impoverished by the expensive war with the Pedi—now saw their fortunes reversed. They

Cetswayo reigned from 1872 to 1879 and was the last king of the Zulu. He traveled to London by ship to plead with the British for the return of Zululand to his people, but his request was denied. ▼

imposed heavy taxes and import duties on the gold-mining industry and charged high prices for services such as water and transportation. With their newfound wealth, the Boers could equip an army. Soon they occupied lands as far north as the Limpopo.

Cecil Rhodes now entered the picture yet again. He believed that there was untapped wealth in the ancient gold mines of the former kingdoms of Rozvi and Monomotapa. These were located in Matabeleland and Mashonaland on the Zimbabwe Plateau. If Rhodes could occupy the area and set up a second gold-mining region there, his British South Africa Company (BSAC)—specially formed for this purpose—would be free of Boer control.

In Matabeleland, Lobengula had succeeded Mzilikazi as the ruler of the Ndebele and

commanded most of the Zimbabwe Plateau. In a truly sinister move, Rhodes's agents deliberately mistranslated a document, tricking Lobengula into granting them the exclusive rights to all mineral deposits in Matabeleland and Mashonaland. The British government awarded Rhodes a charter to colonize the area, and he hastily put his plan into action.

In 1890, Rhodes sent in a heavily armed "pioneer column" of 200 settlers and 500 well-armed BSAC soldiers. They traveled north on the trade route opened up by David Livingstone in the 1840s. Lobengula believed that they were a "work party" passing through his land. In fact, each settler had been promised 15 gold mines and a 1,215-hectare (3,000-acre) farm. After a grueling four-month journey, the settlers arrived, only to find that the mines were almost empty: The

> Lobengula once asked a missionary if he had ever watched a chameleon catching a fly. "The chameleon gets behind the fly, remains motionless for some time, then he advances very slowly and gently, first putting forward one leg and then another. At last, when well within reach, he darts his tongue and the fly disappears. England is the chameleon and I am that fly."

Shona and the Portuguese had already extracted most of the gold. In their search for anything of value, the colonists brutally vandalized the ruins of ancient Zimbabwe and removed many priceless artifacts. Then they staked out farms and began to carve out a living from the African bush.

The settlers were determined to destroy the Ndebele kingdom, and in 1893 they found an excuse to start a full-scale war. Within a few months, their superior firepower had defeated the Ndebele warriors, who never even got close enough to use their *assegais*. Lobengula himself fled and died somewhere in the bush.

The BSAC agents now forced Africans away from the fertile lands settled by Europeans and placed them in poor-quality "reserves." They confiscated the Ndebele's cattle, thus

African workers do most of the heavy labor in South Africa's mining industry today. ▼

removing their source of wealth, their ties to the past, and their means for marriage. They also forced young Ndebele and Shona men to work in the mines and on the farms. In 1895 the new colony, administered by the BSAC and founded by Cecil Rhodes, was named Rhodesia.

Like a series of bad omens, first severe drought and then swarms of locusts destroyed crops in Rhodesia for several years. Then thousands of cattle died of rinderpest, a deadly livestock virus. On the edge of survival, white settlers were horrified when in March 1896 the Ndebele rose in rebellion, followed three months later by the Shona. Both uprisings were unplanned, consisting of many individual acts of violence: a black police officer killed here, a white miner there, a family on a lonely homestead murdered. The Europeans reacted with extra battalions of soldiers and dynamite to blast fugitives out of the caves where they hid. Two Shona spiritual leaders, believed to be ringleaders, were captured and publicly hanged. Today they are considered martyrs in the cause of black freedom.

Although Rhodes had founded a new colony, he had not solved the problems of the mining industry in the Boer republics. Tensions there had been rising for years because the Boers refused to meet British demands for reforms. In the meantime, in the "scramble for Africa," Germany had claimed South-West Africa and Tanganyika (now Namibia and Tanzania). The British government feared an anti-British Boer-German alliance and was also determined to keep the gold mines out of rival European hands. War loomed on the horizon. The British moved in half a million

The spirit medium Kaguvi brought news of the Ndebele uprising back to Mashonaland. The British believed that he was responsible for inciting the Shona rebellion, and publicly hanged him. ▶

troops, and in 1899, the first battles between the British and the Boers took place.

The South African War lasted for three years. Yet, although the Boers suffered total defeat by the British, they afterwards agreed to join forces with their enemy. In 1910 the British colonies and the Boer republics merged as the Union of South Africa. Its main purpose was to ensure white dominance throughout the region.

By the 1950s the South African Afrikaner National Party had developed its notorious system of apartheid, or "separate- ness." The aim of apartheid was to keep Africans under control in poverty-stricken "reserves" while 86 percent of the land was designated "white." In Rhodesia, similar laws kept Africans from voting, forming political parties, becom- ing educated, owning property, or moving freely through the country. But, at the same time, as the British prime minister Harold Macmillan noted, the "winds of change" were sweeping across the continent.

> Doris Lessing, a British writer and Nobel-Prize winner who grew up in Southern Rhodesia during the 1930s, wrote about relationships between white masters and black servants in southern Africa. Charles Mangoshi, a Zimbabwean writer, has published several books and poems about his country, including this one:
>
> *Poised on the thin edge of now*
> *like a poleaxed tightrope walker*
> *the past a roaring lion in the underbrush*
> *the future a nuclear mushroom*
> *I can't swallow.*

Africans had always resisted European colonization and control. When India broke away from Great Britain in 1947, heralding the end of the British Empire, educated African leaders seized this opportunity to continue resistance and demand freedom for their own nations. At the same time, two world wars had changed European attitudes toward the colonies. Now the British planned for "economic and social invest- ment" in their colonies, fol- lowed by eventual African self- government. By the mid- 1960s, after a great deal of fighting and negotiation, most European colonies in Africa had won their independence.

In Rhodesia and South Africa, by contrast, Europeans grimly clung to their power. In Rhodesia it took years of resis- tance, bloodshed, and political maneuvering before African leaders there finally regained command of their own lands in 1980. In recognition of the ancient kingdom on the Plateau, they proudly renamed their free and independent nation Zimbabwe. Where once the great kings of Monomotapa had ruled, Milton Obote (oh BOH te), Zimbabwe's first prime min- ister, now took the reins.

Apartheid

- The Population Registration Act (1950) classified people according to race, dividing them into "white" and "non-white" categories. Non-whites were subdivided into colored (mixed race), Indians (from India), and Bantu (African), with Bantu being further divided into ethnic groups, such as Zulu, Xhosa, and Sotho.

- The Group Areas Act (1950) determined where various races could live.

- The Bantu Education Act (1953) withdrew Africans from missionary education and forced them into government schools, where ethnic differences were emphasized and they were taught only the skills necessary to work for whites.

- These laws were the cornerstones of apartheid, but many other laws controlled relations between the races and laid down guidelines for segregated schools, public places, and transport. African trade unions and other political activities were banned.

In 1990 the entire world celebrated when lawyer and freedom fighter Nelson Mandela was released from 25 years of imprisonment in South Africa. In 1993, after decades of both peaceful and violent resistance, apartheid was finally abolished. And in 1994, Mandela became the country's first black president.

And what of Basutoland, the tiny African-ruled nation floating like an island in the midst of South Africa? The British administered Basutoland as a High Commission Territory, allowing the local chiefs and leaders to rule without interference. However, little money or expertise was invested in the nation, and from the nineteenth century onward, its thriving economy began to decline. Thousands of men and women were forced to seek employment as migrant workers on South African farms and in South African mines and industry. These workers supported the economy of the nation by sending part of their earnings back to Basutoland, as they still do today.

"During my lifetime I have dedicated myself to the struggle of the African people. I have fought against white domination, and I have fought against black domination. I have cherished the ideal of a democratic and free society in which all persons live together in harmony and with equal opportunities. It is an ideal which I hope to live for and to achieve. But if needs be, it is an ideal for which I am prepared to die."
—Nelson Mandela, 1963

In 1966, after three quarters of a century of British administration, Basutoland was granted independence and became the Kingdom of Lesotho. Although Lesotho today has half a million cattle and nearly 3 million sheep, it is one of the world's poorest and least-developed countries. Huge areas of land have been destroyed by overgrazing and the resulting erosion. Certainly this was not how Moshueshue had imagined the future of his nation. Today a statue of Moshueshue stands in Maseru, Lesotho's capital city, as a reminder of the kingdom's founder and his goals.

At last, southern Africa has emerged from the yoke of European colonization. But how much have Western ideas of "civilization" affected the region's indigenous African cultures? Now that they are "independent," can, and should, southern African nations free themselves from the European influences in philosophy, law, religion, language, technology, economics, morals, and—most importantly—the identity that has been imposed upon them for so long?

This is a debate that will occupy modern African leaders in the future—just as it must have occupied the leaders of the past.

◀ A musician from Zimbabwe plays the traditional panpipes.

Pronunciation Key

Some words in this book may be new to you or difficult to pronounce. Those words have been spelled phonetically in parentheses. The syllable that receives stress in a word is shown in small capital letters. The following pronunciation key shows how letters are used to show different sounds.

a	after	(AF tur)	oh	flow	(floh)	ch	chicken	(CHIHK un)
ah	father	(FAH thur)	oi	boy	(boi)	g	game	(gaym)
ai	care	(kair)	oo	rule	(rool)	ing	coming	(KUM ing)
aw	dog	(dawg)	or	horse	(hors)	j	job	(jahb)
ay	paper	(PAY pur)				k	came	(kaym)
			ou	cow	(kou)	ng	long	(lawng)
e	letter	(LET ur)	yoo	few	(fyoo)	s	city	(SIH tee)
ee	eat	(eet)	u	taken	(TAY kun)	sh	ship	(shihp)
				matter	(MAT ur)	th	thin	(thihn)
ih	trip	(trihp)	uh	ago	(uh goh)	thh	feather	(FETHH ur)
eye	idea	(eye DEE uh)				y	yard	(yahrd)
y	hide	(hyd)				z	size	(syz)
ye	lie	(lye)				zh	division	(duh VIHZH un)

For Further Reading

(* = Recommended for younger readers)

Beach, D. N. *The Shona and Zimbabwe, 900–1850*. New York: Africana Publishing, 1980.

Becker, Peter. *Hill of Destiny: The Life and Times of Moshesh*. London: Longman Group, 1969.

Becker, Peter. *Path of Blood: The Rise and Conquests of Mzilikazi*. London: Longman, Green, 1962.

Binns, C. T. *The Last Zulu King: The Life and Death of Cetshwayo*. London: Longman, 1963.

Bourdillon, M. F. C. *The Shona Peoples*. Salisbury, Zimbabwe: Mambo Press, 1976.

Boyd, Herb. *African History for Beginners*. New York: Writers and Readers Publishing, 1991.*

Carpenter, John Allan. *The Enchantment of Africa—Lesotho*. New York: Regensteiner Publishing, 1975.*

Casalis, Eugene. *The Basutos or Twenty-Three Years in South Africa*. London: James Nisbet, 1861.

Casalis, Eugene. *My Life in Basutoland*. Cape Town, South Africa: C. Struik, 1971.

Cheney, Patricia. *The Land and People of Zimbabwe*. New York: J. B. Lippincott, 1990.*

Coates, Austin. *Basutoland*. London: Her Majesty's Stationery Office, 1966.

Cohen, Daniel. *Shaka, King of the Zulus.* New York: Doubleday, 1973.

Cowley, Cecil. *Kwa Zulu: Queen Mkabi's Story.* Cape Town, South Africa: C. Struik, 1966.

Davidson, Basil. *Africa in History.* New York: Macmillan, 1991.

Davidson, Basil. *African Kingdoms.* New York: Time-Life Books, 1966.

Davidson, Basil. *A Guide to African History.* New York: Doubleday, Zenith Books, 1965.

Davidson, Basil. *The Lost Cities of Africa.* Boston: Little, Brown, 1970.

Ellenberger, D. Fred. *History of the Basuto, Ancient and Modern.* New York: Negro Universities Press, 1969.

Fisher, John. *The Afrikaners.* London: Cassell, 1969.

Germond, Robert C. *Chronicles of Basutoland.* Morija-Lesotho, Lesotho: Morija Sesuto Book Depot, 1967.

Garlake, Peter. *The Kingdoms of Africa.* Oxford, England: Elsevier-Phaidon, 1978.

Hall, R. N., and W. G. Neal. *The Ancient Ruins of Rhodesia.* New York: Negro Universities Press, 1969.

Harris, Joseph E. *Africans and Their History.* New York: New American Library, 1987.

Hugon, Anne. *The Exploration of Africa from Cairo to the Cape: Discoveries.* New York: Harry N. Abrams, 1991.

Jenkinson, Thomas B. *Amazulu: The Zulus—Their Past History, Manners, Customs, and Language.* New York: Negro Universities Press, 1969.

Keating, Bern. *Chaka, King of the Zulus.* New York: G. P. Putnam's Sons, 1968.*

Ki-Zerbo, Joseph. *Die Geschichte Schwarz-Afrikas (The History of Black Africa).* Wuppertal, Germany: Peter Hammer, 1979.

Knappert, Jan. *Myths and Legends of Botswana, Lesotho and Swaziland.* Leiden, Germany: E. J. Brill, 1985.

Kunene, Mazisi. *Emperor Shaka the Great: A Zulu Epic.* London: Heinemann, 1979.

Kwamena-Poh, Michael. *African History in Maps.* London: Longman, 1982.

Mallows, Wilfrid. *The Mystery of Great Zimbabwe: A New Solution.* New York: W. W. Norton, 1984.

McEvedy, Collin. *The Penguin Atlas of African History.* London: Penguin Books, 1980.*

Morris, Donald R. *The Washing of the Spears.* New York: Simon and Schuster, 1965.

Mudenge, S.I.G. *A Political History of Munhumutapa, c. 1400–1902.* Harare, Zimbabwe: Zimbabwe Publishing House, 1988.

Murray, Jocelyn. *Cultural Atlas of Africa.* New York: Facts on File, 1989.*

Oliver, Roland. *The African Experience.* New York: HarperCollins, 1991.

Oliver, Roland. *The Dawn of African History.* London: Oxford University Press, 1968.

Oliver, Roland, and J. D. Fage. *A Short History of Africa.* 6th ed. London: Penguin Books, 1988.

O'Toole, Thomas. *Zimbabwe in Pictures.* Minneapolis: Lerner Publications, 1988.*

Ritter, E. A. *Shaka Zulu: The Rise of the Zulu Empire.* London: Longman, Green, 1955.

Sanders, Peter. *Moshoeshoe, Chief of the Sotho.* London: Heinemann Educational Books, 1975.

Saunders, Christopher. *Black Leaders in Southern Africa's History.* London: Heinemann Educational Books, 1979.

Scholefield, A. *The Dark Kingdoms.* New York: William Morrow, 1975.

Stacey, Tom. *Peoples of the Earth.* Tom Stacey and Europa, 1972.*

Stanley, Diane, and Peter Venemma. *Shaka, King of the Zulus.* New York: Morrow Junior Books, 1988.*

Stevens, Richard P. *Lesotho, Botswana, and Swaziland.* New York: Frederick A. Praeger, 1963.

Tedder, Vivian. *The People of a Thousand Hills.* Cape Town, South Africa: C. Struik, 1968.*

Theal, George McCall. *Records of South-Eastern Africa.* Cape Town, South Africa: C. Struik, 1964.

Tonsing-Carter, Betty. *Lesotho.* New York: Chelsea House, 1988.*

Tracey, Hugh. *Antonio Fernandes, Discoverer of Monomotapa.* Lisbon, Portugal: Historical Archives of Mozambique, 1940.

Tylden, G. *The Rise of the Basuto.* Cape Town, South Africa: Juta, 1950.

Villet, Barbara. *Blood River.* New York: Everest House, 1982.

Webb, C. de B., and J. B. Wright. *A Zulu King Speaks.* Pietermaritzburg, Natal: University of Natal Press, 1978.

Index